Cooking with Belgian Beers

Great recipes flavoured with the famous 'Westhoek' beers

Chef Stefaan Couttenye from 't Hommelhof in Watou

Recipes • Stefaan Couttenye, Beer suggestions • Simon Couttenye
Texts • Jan Dhondt, Photos • Tom Swijns

stichting kunstboek

Table of Contents

All dishes are intended for 4 persons, unless otherwise stated.

A thriving habitat

Flanders’ Fields

The country has recovered.

Within the triangle of De Panne in the West, Middelkerke in the East and Wervik in the South, there are 95 sleepy villages with weird and wonderful names, like Lampernisse, Gyverinkhove, Mannekensvere…
They are peppered around like the dots on a red toadstool: Flanders’ Fields, our country’s best kept secret. Presumably, your thoughts automatically turn to ‘The Great War’ as the global madness of 1914-1918 is still being deferentially referred to here. It comes as no surprise, therefore, that the landscape is still carrying numerous scars, with its hundreds of military cemeteries, where victims from all continents were united in death. But there is so much more. The country has recovered. The locals’ dogged determination and work etiquette are legendary, and so it is that today, you will come across a thriving environment where life is particularly good. And in no time at all, you will discover that behind the disarming modesty of the locals lurks generous hospitality.

Flanders’ Fields can boast assets like de *Schreve,* the sea, *de Moeren,* the ‘Mountains’ and panoramic vistas. Agriculture is on a small scale, and many farms work in a traditional manner. Even when it comes to relaxation, you’ve come to the right place in Flanders’ Fields, with its renowned music festivals, international art happenings, great theme parks, endless cycling and walking routes, fascinating museums, miles of water fun and in addition to all of this, more gastronomic treasures per square kilometre than in any other region (leaving Paris aside).

The historical significance of Flanders' Fields cannot be underestimated.

For a long time, this backwater was considered the kingdom's misfit, and you were hard pushed to find a better bargaining chip for boundary disputes. It was, in historical order, the Romans, the Franks, the Spanish, the Austrians, the French and the Dutch who ruled the roost, all of whom left their mark. It was here that the Beggars (Protestant noblemen led by Willem of Orange) took a swipe at history, and Pope Innocent X was given tit for tat. Here, Iconoclasm raged in full force, Alva let loose his bloodhounds and witch hunts were at their peak. Ironically, it is precisely the many occupiers and the often horrific oppression which formed the national identity and ensured that many traditions were preserved. Sometimes, it seems as if you are going back in time. That is certainly the case when you cross the *'Schreve'*, which is what the French border is referred to here.
The names are Flemish, the streets look familiar, the local dishes are related and if you listen carefully, Flemish people do not need a dictionary to understand the conversations of the older locals. Some knowledge of the West Flemish dialect is a bonus, but not a must, as you will get by anyhow without difficulty.

The West Coast boasts the country's widest beaches. Behind them lies an even wider dune section of 640 acres which, in terms of nature reserve, has no equal in Flanders. The reserve has a micro climate, making it eminently suitable for the sweet burnet rose, the dune pansy, Sheep's bit scabious, grey hair-grass and reindeer lichen to thrive. Unlike the coastal cities past the *Nieuwpoort Ganzenpoot*, tourism here is on a human scale. There is little or no mass tourism, and more than enough room to breathe. In the vast *Moeren*, you face an endless wind and an audible silence. At one time, the whole area was under water, but hard-working monks laid it dry.
As a result, the most fertile polder soil surfaced and endless pastures guarantee top-quality dairy produce.
Historical towns like Nieuwpoort, Diksmuide, Veurne, Ieper and Poperinge, which have been carefully restored or rebuilt, provide an extensive range of goods and services.
In Heuvelland, farmers are even trying their hand at viticulture now, and 'border trade' flourishes like nowhere else. This is why a Picon tastes at its most divine in a pavement cafe on the *Rode Berg*. In clear weather, you can even overlook the entire region from a cable car.
From here, Mesen, Belgium's smallest town, is only a hop, skip and a jump away. With its 950 inhabitants, it is living proof that language facilities work.
And then there are the many forests that are, more often than not, steeped in dark mystery: the *Vrijbos*, where Ludovicus Baekelandt hid with his robbers, the *Nonnenbossen* which was teeming with witches and the *Helleketelbos* [Hell Cauldron Forest] which speaks for itself …
You cannot really grow weary of Flanders' Fields. In fact, the biggest problem you will face is when you can plan your next holiday? You can stay at one of the many holiday farms, picturesque hotels or cosy B&Bs, of which there are now hundreds.

‘t Hommelhof

Both earnest and fun

Some buildings look so natural that it seems as if they never started life on a drawing board but grew organically on the spot. They form part of the street scene, much like the stars in the sky, and will be a reassuring anchoring point until the end of time. In Watou, there is the village square, the statue of the dead, the church, the village hall and …’t Hommelhof: white-washed walls, lush greenery and soft neon light.

In the 17th century, the building began its prestigious life as a tavern of brewery *Sint-Joris* and law courts of the *Cortewylle* estate. Earnestness and fun under one and the same roof. It proved a golden formula, for anyone who was convicted could drown their sorrows next-door, and anyone who was acquitted did not have to walk far to celebrate. For years, ‘t Hommelhof, which was since renamed ‘Bij Désiré Devos’ carried on its merry way as an obvious meeting place and local news agent.
Watou was little affected by the ‘Big World Fires’, and this is how the quiet border village made it to the middle of last century pretty much unscathed, and was able to face burgeoning tourism head-on. From then on, eating was called ‘savouring’ and cookery became ‘gastronomy’. Chefs were launched into stardom and made it to the cover of glossy magazines without any problems at all. Sports icons and rock & roll legends met with stiff competition, but where their fame usually has a limited shelf life, chefs carve out a career for themselves which does not end until the last customer has left.

Following an interim period as a dance cafe, which drew in mainly French people, ‘t Hommelhof made its comeback as a restaurant and focused on regional gastronomy from the outset. The name inspired the kitchen, and beer-based dishes became its trademark. Quite a few ornaments in the rustic context refer to the labour-intensive hops. No sophisticated or design seating, but dead simple pluckers’ seats. Hop vines hanging from the beams, worn out floor boards, antique furniture and vintage ornaments take you back to a by-gone era when the living was easy and the word ‘stress’ had yet to be invented. Whether you like it or not, you automatically switch down a gear, which only benefits the enjoyment.

Here, the seasons are respected rigorously.

Exquisite food is served in a semi-sacred atmosphere, and every creation is matched by a suitable brew in the cellar. Here, the seasons are respected rigorously, and so you should not expect asparagus in the middle of winter. There is game in the autumn and lots of stews in winter. Fresh hop shoots herald spring and lavish salads appear on the menu in summer. Needless to say, tried-and-tested classics also feature on the menu, but then with a twist so that they can be rediscovered all over again.

The ingredients are sourced locally as much as possible, something which does not only benefit freshness and quality, it also makes for a taste sensation which bland fast-food or industrial meals can only dream of. The tartness of watercress or crunchy radishes, the intense satisfaction of oven-fresh farmer's bread with a lump of lard, the salty finesse of freshly-prepared lobster or the warm sensation of ham that melts like butter ... paradise served on a platter!

The kitchen may be the restaurant's nerve centre, hospitality is as much an art. In 't Hommelhof, your wish is taken seriously and suggestions are gratefully accepted. Customers often end up friends here, and anyone who's anyone in Belgium has been known to eat in this establishment. Even the royal family is included in 't Hommelhof's address book.
The many artists who have graced the Arts Festival with their presence have left their artistic mark in many of the artefacts or literary outpourings, very often with a hidden wink to 't Hommelhof. Nothing can beat, of course, an aperitif under the grapevine in the courtyard on a sunny day, or a flowery street terrace where you can see life in a Flanders' Fields village go by at its leisurely pace. Moreover, 't Hommelhof is strategically placed for all those who have a major outing in mind: hikers and cyclists can revel in nature which is at its most beautiful in this part of the country. Historical towns, with all manner of museums, are within easy travelling distance, and even those who want to fool around in a theme park first need not travel for miles to finish their day in style.

2011
MICHELIN Gids
STEFAAN
COUTTENYE

Two generations

Beer, local product *par excellence*, has been given an epic starring role.

If obstinacy and determination were qualities, then Stefaan Couttenye would definitely be a medal winner. A heavyweight who's turned his back on city life to return to his roots? Not exactly an everyday occurrence. You cannot deny your roots, though, and so his West-Flemish dialect has a slightly exotic accent which gives his bonhomie extra shine. When he decided to let his fate be guided by Catering College Ter Duinen in Koksijde, the usual obstacles needed to be negotiated, but masterly plans for the future by his parents, paralysing nostalgia or distant relocations could not quench the sacred fire. After his studies, there were the work placements, and that is how Stefaan ended up with Marc Paesbrugghe in the renowned 'Sir Anthony Van Dijck'. That is where the proverbial scales fell from his eyes, and where he gained the insight that those who want to cook must go back to basics. Without proper product knowledge, there cannot be an appreciation of taste, and without an appreciation of taste, there cannot be virtuosity. There is absolutely no doubt that virtuosity is needed to get to the essence of a product. Like no other, Stefaan manages to break down classic dishes, only to reconstruct them, having added his highly personal interpretation.

Of course, 't Hommelhof was temporarily fascinated by fashionable trends, but that is all they remained: a temporary fascination. Solidity, craftsmanship and creativity are the mainstays, although beer, the local produce *par excellence,* has been given an epic starring role. Just about all the local brews have been tested for their usefulness, and the surprising combinations that this has brought about are quite stunning. Infusions, syrups, marinades and sauces ... there is always a hint of hops or a malty touch which stimulates the taste buds with an indefinable treat. At times contrasting, while in perfect harmony at other times, but always divine. Beer kitchen has become a household concept, a quirky formula to expand the gastronomic panorama endlessly.

Beer Pairing tip

And then there's the son ...

Not a rattle or blocks for little Simon, no, but give him a spatula, a whisk and a casserole, and he'd be drumming away happily for hours! Anyone who has spent his childhood between pots and pans is at risk of a serious infection with the culinary virus! And recovery is not straightforward, whether you like it or not. Simon was no exception. As it was in the nature of things, when the time was right, he attended the Catering College Ter Duinen in Koksijde, where he completed the curriculum with a seventh year of beverage knowledge as a valuable added bonus. Before he put his knowledge and expertise to the test at home, he worked as a wine waiter with numerous renowned chefs, including Kobe Desramaults at 'In de Wulf ' in Dranouter.

The key to the success of any restaurant is a good division of labour, and so it was clear from the outset that Simon would assist his father as host and drinks specialist. Needless to say, a beer restaurant requires a palette that is different from a place with an extensive wine list, and that is the reason Simon attended a 'beer brewing' course at Syntra in Ieper. The restaurant's private kitchen was emptied, and barrels and brewing kettles were brought in. And within no time at all, brewing bubbling and frothing beer was no longer a pastime but an outright passion. The production is deliberately kept to a minimum, which allows 't Hommelhof to come up with a number of exclusive brews, with 'Frambley' as its leading brew for the time being. In the meantime, Simon employs his youthful charm and sound knowledge to guarantee every customer a gourmet experience with a drink to match.

Hop shoots from ‘t Hoppecruyt

For anyone who has tasted them once, spring cannot come quickly enough.

Whilst hops are used the world over, not every region is suitable for growing them. It so happens that the border region of Flanders' Fields is eminently suited for this. Indeed, thanks to a mild maritime climate, the plant manages to develop very rich and unique flavours.
The complexity of the hops (here they call it *hommel*) is nowhere else so interesting, but this is, of course, also thanks to the sandy loam soil where the roots find what they need. Hop vines need a great deal of moisture, and the Flemish soil ensures that the moisture is easily absorbed, but can, if need be, also be stored for longer periods of time. However, there are so many aspects that are out of your control, that you need to intervene from time to time in order to grow a decent crop. Growers have absolutely no control over what the rain carries with it, and we cannot imagine what substances are in the atmosphere. So it is mainly a matter of protecting the crops from polluting substances for which others are responsible. Insects are controlled organically. Weed control is completely mechanical and, to a large extent, done by hand. Even though this requires a lot of hard work, the satisfaction you get from seeing the vines climb up day after day is priceless.

Young shoots with character

The hop cones are brought to the brewery in their entirety, but in spring, first-class hop shoots are also offered for sale now. Previously, these shoots were discarded, or at best eaten by the farmer himself. Since their gastronomic qualities have been discovered, they are sold in spring as a true delicacy.

For anyone who has tasted them once, spring cannot come quickly enough, because this crunchy delicacy strictly adheres to the seasons. If you want to find out more about the crop and its many applications, including medicinal, feel free to visit the company. 't Hoppecruyt has been going strong for four generations, and given the growing success of local produce, this is not about to end any time soon.

't Hoppecruyt
Wout en Benedikte Desmyter-Coutigny
Provenplein 69
8972 Poperinge (Proven), Belgium
Tel: +32 (0)57/30.05.98
www.hoppecruyt.be

Calf's head with quail's eggs, fresh hop shoots and Paulus-infused mayonnaise

Calf's head

1 calf's head split into two, tongue included
5 l well-flavoured bouillon
3 l spicy tomato sauce
fresh garden herbs: basil, rosemary, marjoram, thyme, laurel, sage and tarragon
500 g mushrooms
100 g green, pitted olives
100 g gherkins
250 g minced veal
(rolled into small balls)
½ l Paulus

The preparation beforehand is rather involved.
One calf's head will feed about 20 people.
You can also get prepared calf's head from your local butcher, of course.

- Allow the head and tongue to soak in cold, salted water overnight. Drain the head, rinse thoroughly and leave it to boil in a well-flavoured bouillon for two hours.
- Pick the meat from the bones, chop it finely and mix it in with the spicy tomato sauce to which fresh garden herbs have been added.
- Add a garnish of chopped and sautéed mushrooms, the chopped gherkins, olives and meatballs. Bring to the boil and add the beer.
- Pour into a suitable dish and leave to rest for a few days.

Preparation per 400 g calf's head

80 g hop shoots
8 quail's eggs
5 cl vinegar
1/2 small butternut squash
50 g butter
50 g shiso mix (young shoots)
a piping bag

- Clean the hop shoots one by one: remove the hard ends so that you are left with the 5 to 7 cm long meaty section.
- Poach the quail's eggs for one minute in boiling salt water with vinegar and leave them to cool.
- Peel the butternut, remove the seeds and cut into chunks. Cook in some water with salt and pepper. Drain and add butter to attain a smooth mixture. Allow the butternut cream to cool before placing it in a piping bag or espuma bottle.

Mayonnaise

10 cl Paulus
4 eggs
1 tbsp natural vinegar
1 tbsp mustard
1 tbsp warm water
4 dl peanut oil

- Allow the beer to reduce to a syrup-like consistency. Allow to cool and beat the egg yolks in it.
- Add the vinegar, water and mustard.
- Add the peanut oil, drop by drop, while stirring constantly. Season the mayonnaise with salt and pepper and put it in a piping bag or espuma bottle.

Presentation

- Place two slices of calf's head on the plate.
- Arrange the hop shoots and shiso around them.
- Pipe dollops of mayonnaise and butternut cream on the plate and garnish with the quail's eggs.

Beer Pairing tip

Paulus
Het Sas Brewery, Boezinge
Old Brown

Summery drinking beer.
Sweet and tart, full of character.
A traditional dish requires dark confidence in the glass.

Mousse of organic chicken from Zillebeke and Papegaei, salad of fresh hop shoots and lemon mayonnaise

Preparation

1 organic chicken
1 leek
1 celery stalk
1 carrot
1 onion
2 bay leaves
1 sprig of thyme
2 cloves
5 sheets of gelatine
25 cl double cream
6 slices of chicken breast
1 narrow, tall terrine mould

- Place the chicken with the roughly chopped vegetables and herbs in a pot with plenty of water and leave them to simmer just under boiling point for one hour. Regularly skim off the scum rising to the surface.
- Remove the chicken from the bouillon, remove the skin and pick the meat from the bones.
- Drain the bouillon in a fine sieve.
- Blend the chicken meat and ½ litre of bouillon.
- Add the soaked and squeezed gelatine.
- Cool down to room temperature.
- Fold the half-whipped cream under the mixture.
- Line the flat bottom of the mould with cling film, arrange the slices of chicken breast side by side on the film and pour the mousse over it.
- Allow to set in the refrigerator for a few hours until it feels firm.
- Cut into cubes just before serving.

Jelly

10 cl Papegaei
25 cl bouillon
juice of ½ lemon
4 sheets of gelatine

- Bring the 25 cl of clarified bouillon, the Papegaei and the lemon juice to the boil.
- Stir the soaked and squeezed gelatine sheets in the hot liquid.
- Pour the jelly into a flat dish and allow to set in the refrigerator.
- Mash the jelly with a fork just before serving.

Lemon mayonnaise

4 egg yolks
juice of 1 lemon
1 tbsp mustard
4 dl peanut oil

- Beat the egg yolks briefly and stir in the lemon juice and mustard.
- Add the oil, drop by drop, and continue to stir.
- Season with salt and pepper.
- You can make the mayonnaise more runny by adding extra lemon juice or water.

Presentation

a few leaves of dandelion salad
1 lemon

- Arrange 3 cubes of mousse on a chilled plate, with the chicken breast facing up.
- Spread a few spoonfuls of jelly on the plate.
- Pipe a few tufts of lemon mayonnaise between the cubes and finish off with slices of lemon and leaves of dandelion salad.

Beer Pairing tip

Papegaei
Verstraete Brewery, Diksmuide
Blond

Mellow fresh onset of Proven hops with a fruity aftertaste. The silky-smooth mousse combines effortlessly with the crisp tartness of the hop shoots thanks to the tangy Papegaei.

Scallops with *witte pens* (tripe), cauliflower, dried ham and hop shoots in Westvleteren Blond

200 g hop shoots
2 slices fresh ham
½ cauliflower
100 g butter
10 cl Westvleteren Blond
10 cl fish fond or stock
1 shallot
1 *witte pens* (tripe) from Veurne
8 scallops (only the white meat)
5 cl peanut oil
1 tbsp hazelnut oil

Preparation

- Rinse the shoots in lemon water and break off the woody ends.
- Allow the ham slices to dry in the oven (3 hours at 85 °C with the oven door ajar).
- Allow the cauliflower florets to simmer in cold, salted water for 15 minutes. Drain them well.
  Blend them with a knob of butter, season with salt and pepper, and keep them warm.
- Allow the beer and fish stock, together with a finely chopped shallot, to reduce to one-third of its original volume. Remove the pot from the hob, mix cubes of butter into the sauce and keep it warm.
- Cut the tripe into 8 equal pieces and dab the ends with peanut oil.
- Season the scallops with salt and pepper and fry them on both sides for one minute in peanut oil.
- Fry the fresh hop shoots briefly with a knob of butter and season with salt and pepper. Spoon the hazelnut oil over the shoots .

Presentation

Arrange everything neatly on a hot plate and drizzle the sauce in between.

Beer Pairing tip

Trappist Westvleteren Blond
Sint-Sixtus Brewery, Westvleteren
Abbey Beer

Punchy, malty, fresh and fruity in taste. Very pleasant hoppy accent. The scallops share their salty finesse with the fresh promise of balanced acids.

Young birds with character

La maison Flandre Pigeonneau

Just across the border

Whilst the man in the street had to make do with a pigeon at the end of its career, the middle and upper classes would feast on the young specimens that were about to spread their wings and explore the world. In other words, until the middle of last century, this delicacy was something the common people just could not afford. If you now read what the Chinese are prepared to pay for them, you will think twice about frying a *columbida* (as the biologists refer to them) with a lump of butter ... And that is a shame. Nothing beats a tender pigeon! Luckily, Alex Dequidt decided to start his own pigeon-breeding farm with the sole intention of providing the fans what they wanted. No competitions, no trophies, no medals, just a delicious piece of meat! Just across the border, in Steenvoorde, Alex started with 64 pigeon couples from the Tarn region (South Pyrenees) 25 years ago with a view to achieving the most appropriate bird thanks to extensive selection. Meanwhile, he now has 4,000 couples that guarantee some 1,000 mature birds, ready for slaughter, every week. All of them are surrounded with the same care and love as the pioneers which they started out with. Accordingly, the pigeons enjoy relative freedom in the immense, south-west-facing cages, and are only fed the best grain and corn from the region.

After four weeks, they are ready for slaughter. Everything is done naturally, and the entire process is purely traditional. In order to guarantee the quality of the finished product, the animals are slaughtered and prepared for cooking on the spot. In that way, the birds need not endure any stress, which only benefits the meat. Many chefs from renowned restaurants have found their way to Steenvoorde and do not hesitate to give the pigeons pride of place on their menus. Meanwhile, the company has burst beyond its seams to the extent that both sons Julien and Rémi have come onboard to make sure that this delicacy remains available for a long time to come.

Flandre pigeonneau
Alex Dequidt
350 route de Bailleul
Steenvoorde (FR)
Tel: +33 (0)848 16 71

Pigeon in a puff pastry with foie gras and Westvleteren 12

½ red cabbage
½ onion
2 tbsp lard
1 stewing apple
50 g sugar
1 tbsp vinegar
1 sprig of thyme
1 bay leaf
4 pigeons
25 g butter
25 cl brown fond
(see fillet of polder hare p.132)
5 cl Westvleteren 12
4 sheets of puff pastry
100 g foie gras

Preparation

- Cut the cabbage into thin strips and finely chop the onion. Heat the lard in a pan, fry the chopped onion briefly (do not let it turn brown).
- Peel the apple, remove the core, cut into small pieces and add to the red cabbage. Sprinkle with sugar and add vinegar.
  Add thyme, bay leaf, salt and pepper and leave to simmer for an hour.
- Allow the pigeon breasts to brown briefly with butter in the pan, and place them in the refrigerator.
- Brown the legs and wings in butter, allow them to cook for 5 minutes and place them in the refrigerator.
- Deglaze the pan with the fond and the beer and allow the sauce to reduce to a syrup-like consistency.
- Place the sheets of puff pastry on a baking tray. Place two legs/wings symmetrically in the centre of a pastry sheet on a baking tray and place on each leg/wing a breast.
  Place a sheet of pastry on top of the breasts and close the parcels in order to mimic the shape of a pigeon.
  Bake the pigeons in a pre-heated oven at 190 °C for 12 minutes.

Presentation

- Put some red cabbage in the centre of a hot plate and arrange the pigeons on top.
- Drizzle the sauce around it.

Beer Pairing tip

Trappist Westvleteren 12
Sint-Sixtus Brewery, Westvleteren
Dark Trappist

Full, creamy aroma. Rich caramelised and malty flavours.

Young pigeon from Steenvoorde in St. Bernardus Prior 8, with a pea puree and asparagus

Preparation the day before

4 young pigeons
coarsely chopped onion, carrot and celery
10 cl St. Bernardus Prior 8 (Brown Abbey Ale)
50 cl brown fond
1 bay leaf
1 sprig of thyme
Panko bread crumbs
100 g peas (fresh or frozen)
50 g butter
1 bundle of white asparagus
1 pinch of sugar

- Remove the pigeons from their carcasses (or ask your poulterer to do this for you).
- Brown the bones in a knob of butter with the coarsely chopped onion, carrot and celery.
- Add the beer and half of the brown fond.
  Add thyme and the bay leaf and allow the bones to simmer for some two hours.
- Pour through a chinois sieve and catch the bouillon.
- Briefly sauté the legs/wings in a knob of butter and allow them to cook with some bouillon for some 20 minutes.
- Remove the meat from the bones, blend with some bouillon and allow to cool in the refrigerator.

Preparation on the day

- Make balls with the cooled meat and roll them in the panko bread crumbs.
- Boil the peas in salted water for half a minute and immediately rinse them in icy cold water to make sure they retain their fresh green colour.
  Replace on the hob with a splash of water and a knob of butter and cook for another 10 minutes.
- Mash them with a hand blender until you end up with a smooth consistency.
- Peel the asparagus and top and tail them.
  Cut the asparagus into discs and fry them in some butter.
  Season with pepper, salt and a pinch of sugar.
- Allow the pigeon breasts to fry in browned butter until crisp and deglaze the pan with the rest of the fond. Reduce to a thick sauce-like consistency.
- Allow the breasts to bake for another 4 minutes or so in a pre-heated oven at 180 °C. Allow them to rest for 5 minutes in a warm place.
  They should be nice and pink.
- Fry the meat balls.

Presentation

- Create with the back of a spoon 'tears' of pea puree on the plate.
- Arrange the asparagus, sliced breast and meat balls on top.
- Drizzle the sauce on top.

Beer Pairing tip

St. Bernardus Prior 8
St. Bernardus Brewery, Watou
Belgian Abbey Ale

Malt-fruity, full-bodied flavour and sweet-bitter aftertaste. The beer's subdued flexibility complements the juiciness of the young game well.

Salad of young pigeon with Frambley (1/3) versus Weltmerz (2/3)

4 pigeons
25 g butter
mixed salad (red and white crisp, oak leaf, radicchio)
1 tbsp pine nuts
1 tbsp hazelnuts
1 tbsp pistachio nuts

2,5 cl Frambley
5 cl Weltmerz
1 tbsp white wine vinegar
1 tsp mustard
10 cl olive oil

Young pigeon

- Allow the breasts and legs/wings to brown in butter and season with salt and pepper.
- Leave them to bake in a pre-heated oven for 3 minutes at 180 °C.
- Remove the breasts from the oven and keep them warm. Leave the legs/wings to cook for another 10 minutes.

Vinaigrette

- Put all the ingredients for the vinaigrette into the blender and mix them well.

Presentation

- Arrange the salad on a plate and drizzle with vinaigrette.
- Cut up the breasts, remove the meat from the bones and divide the meat over the lettuce.
- Sprinkle with nuts.

Beer Pairing tip

Frambley
Simco 't Hommelhof Brewery, Watou
Fruit Beer

Bitter-sweet onset with subtly tangy aftertaste.

Weltmerz
Struise Brouwers Brewery, Oostvleteren
Sour Ale

Fresh, pleasant acidity, the perfect beer to enjoy on a terrace on a hot summer's day. The relatively high acidity level is almost similar to that of the Geuze. The young pigeon transforms a grim duel into a harmonious *pas-de-deux*.

St. Bernardus®
Watou
Hemelse nectar binnen handbereik

With home-grown hops

St. Bernardus Brewery

That monk still has one foot in the door.

Zythologists can hardly keep up, because every day, a new brew is poured onto the market, one better than the other. One could be forgiven to think that brewing is not just about knowhow, but just as much about tradition. As far as the latter is concerned, St. Bernardus Brewery can present excellent credentials. When the monks of Westvleteren stopped brewing commercially shortly after World War II, they found a willing partner in the then St. Bernard dairy in Watou to continue brewing and selling under licence. Their brewmaster, Mathieu Szafranski (of Polish origin), was prepared to relocate and brought, along with his knowledge, the original recipes and the original Saint-Sixtus yeast. The new brand was named 'Trappist Westvleteren', 'St. Sixtus' and later on just 'Sixtus'. Until 1992, everything went well, and Sixtus became a moderate success, but when the licence expired and the monks decided to resume their commercial activity, however, the brewery in Watou needed to change its label.

St Bernardus
Prior 8

The name became 'St. Bernardus', but since the beer could no longer be sold as a Trappist beer, the monk on the label had to go, and was replaced by a profane, bold-headed old man with no crucifix around his neck. The beer stayed exactly the same, but the clerical layer disappeared.
Now, more than 20 years later, St. Bernardus stands for quality beers that scoop many prizes worldwide. They only work with their own home-grown hops, and yeast is obviously a major factor in this, along with the water from an ancient source, which is a priceless asset. The range has been extended substantially, and that is why today, there are no fewer than 8 different beers to choose from. You may be spoilt for choice, but the reward is always heavenly. And so the monk still has one foot in the door.

St. Bernardus Brewery
Trappistenweg 23
8978 Watou, Belgium
Tel: +32 (0)57 38 80 21
www.sintbernardus.be

Artichoke with seafood, baby spinach and a lobster sauce with St. Bernardus Tripel

Beer Pairing tip

St. Bernardus Tripel
St. Bernardus Brewery, Watou
Belgian Abbey Ale

Flowery, fruity aroma, bitter-sweet balance, steady aftertaste. The salty accents, suitably set off by the fruity touches, allow the basic character of the artichoke to blossom.

Bisque

½ kg shrimp shells
1 tbsp olive oil
1 onion
1 carrot
½ green celery
1 clove of garlic
1 sprig of thyme
1 bay leaf
1 tbsp flour
1 tbsp tomato puree
25 cl chicken fond
cayenne pepper

- Allow the shrimp shells to discolour over a high heat in some olive oil.
- Add the finely chopped vegetables (onion, carrot, celery) and the herbs (thyme, bay leaf, garlic) and sauté these briefly.
- Sprinkle the mixture with flour and stir in the tomato puree. Allow all the moisture to be absorbed.
- Add the chicken fond and cook for 20 minutes whilst stirring to prevent burning.
- Pour the *bisque* through a sieve and season with salt and cayenne pepper.

Preparation

4 artichokes
½ lemon
100 g monkfish fillet
4 scampi
1 tbsp peanut oil
4 langoustines
10 cl St. Bernardus Tripel
250 g baby spinach
1 knob of butter
100 g peeled shrimps
25 g butter

- Rinse the artichokes under cold water and break off the stems.
- Place the artichokes with half a lemon (to preserve the fresh colour) in a pot of cold, salted water and cook for 45 minutes. Place during cooking a plate on the artichokes to ensure that they remain under water. Insert a fork into the base. If it meets no resistance, they are done.
- Remove the artichokes from the water, drain them upside down and remove the centre leaves and any loose fibres. Place them on a warm plate.
- Stir-fry the monkfish and scampi in the peanut oil and add the unpeeled langoustines right at the end. Allow them to cook on both sides for two minutes.
- Allow the fried monkfish and scampi to cook some more in the *bisque* with beer. Keep the langoustines as garnish for later.
- Sauté the spinach in a knob of butter.

Presentation

- Divide the spinach over the artichoke hearts. Use deep plates for this dish.
- Place the fish with *bisque* on top of the spinach and arrange a langoustine and shrimps around it.

Mousse of Ganda ham with Watou Tripel

1½ gelatine sheets
75 g Ganda ham
40 g boiled ham
10 cl semi-whipped cream
½ Cavaillon melon
200 g water melon
5 cl Watou Tripel
4 slices dried Ganda ham
4 crackers

Preparation

- Soak the gelatine sheets in cold water.
- Remove the rind and fat from the ham, shred the ham and bring to the boil with 1 dl of water.
  Blend the water and ham and stir in the squeezed gelatine sheets.
- Fold the semi-whipped cream under the mixture, pour into a tall dish and leave to set in the refrigerator.
- Make balls of the Cavaillon and water melons (2 of each per person) and mix up the rest of the fruit flesh with the beer.

Presentation

- Pour a splash of melon coulis into a cold, deep plate and arrange 2 cubes of ham mousse on top.
- Garnish with the melon balls and some fresh herbs.
- Insert a cracker and dried Ganda slice into the mousse.

Beer Pairing tip

Watou Tripel
St.Bernardus Brewery, Watou
Belgian Abbey Ale

Flowery, fruity flavour, sweet bitter harmony, well-balanced aftertaste.
The delicate salty flavour of the meat is highlighted by the summery onset of the beer.

Vol-au-vent with sweetbreads and Oosterschelde lobster in St. Bernardus Wit

Lobster and sweetbreads

1 carrot
1 stalk of celery
1 onion
1 leek
1 Oosterschelde lobster
(500 g live weight)
200 g sweetbreads (of the heart)
thyme, bay leaf

- Clean the vegetables and cut them up into large chunks. Put half of them into a large pot with 5 l of water, season and bring to the boil.
- Place the lobster, with the head forward, into the boiling water and allow to simmer for 10 minutes.
- Allow the lobster to cool down in the liquid. Remove the armour.
- Blanch the sweetbreads in boiling, salted water and immediately cool them down in ice water.
- Then let them simmer for 20 minutes in salted water with the rest of the chopped vegetables, thyme and bay leaf.
- Allow the sweetbreads to cool down in the liquid. Remove the membranes.

Filling

25 cl chicken stock
10 cl St. Bernardus Wit
25 cl cream
1 egg yolk
lemon juice
2 chicken breasts from Zillebeke
3 knobs of butter
the lobster and sweetbreads
200 g beech mushrooms

- Reduce the stock and beer to half its original volume. Add the cream and once again, reduce by half. Remove the pot from the hob, add the egg yolk and season with salt and pepper. Drizzle with some lemon juice for a fresh touch.
- Char the chicken breasts in a knob of butter, then bake for half an hour in a pre-heated oven at 90 °C. Warm up the lobster and sweetbreads by adding them to the chicken for the last 10 minutes.
- Cut the chicken, sweetbreads and lobster in small pieces.
- Sauté the mushrooms in a knob of butter.
- Mix a knob of butter into the cream sauce and mix it with the rest of the filling.

Puff pastry biscuits

4 slices of puff pastry
1 egg
brush
cutter

- Beat the egg with a little water and cut for one biscuit one disk from the puff pastry.
- Brush all disks with egg for a shiny look. Bake them 15 to 20 minutes until golden brown in a pre-heated oven at 180 °C.
- Cut all the biscuits in half. This way, you get a jar with a lid.

Mousseline sauce

2 egg yolks
50 g melted butter
juice of ½ lemon
nutmeg
cayenne pepper

- Place all the ingredients in a pot over a low heat.
- Beat into a fluffy mousseline consistency and season with cayenne pepper, salt and nutmeg.

Presentation

- Scoop a large spoonful of filling on and around the bottom half of the biscuit and cover with the top half.
- Finish off with the mousseline sauce and garnish with sprigs of chervil.

Beer Pairing tip

St. Bernardus Wit
St. Bernardus Brewery, Watou
White Beer

Light and refreshing.
The hint of acidity is in perfect harmony with a creamy sensation.

Guinea fowl fillet from Zillebeke, *confit* of the leg, shrimps and hop shoots in St. Bernardus Pater 6

Sauce (can be prepared the day before)

1 kg fresh shrimp shells
dash of olive oil
1 onion
1 carrot
½ green celery
1 clove of garlic
cayenne pepper
1 bay leaf
1 sprig of thyme
1 tbsp tomato puree
1 tbsp flour
25 cl chicken fond

- Let the shells discolour over a high heat in some olive oil.
- Add thyme, bay leaf, cayenne pepper and the finely chopped onion, carrot, celery and garlic. Allow to cook for a few minutes before adding the flour and tomato puree. Wait until all the moisture has been absorbed, whilst stirring constantly, over a low heat.
- Add the chicken fond, continue stirring and allow the mixture to simmer for 20 minutes. Stir occasionally to make sure the flour does not stick; add a splash of water when the mixture is too dry.
- Pass the sauce through a fine mesh and season.

Guinea fowl

2 fine guinea fowl
80 g butter
25 cl St. Bernardus Pater 6
50 cl brown fond
1 kg peeled shrimps
(unpeeled weight)

- Bone the guinea fowl and cut fillets from the carcass.
- The bones are used to make the *confit*:
  Brown all over in a knob of browned butter.
  Cover with half the beer and fond and allow to simmer in a pre-heated oven for some 45 minutes at 150 °C.
  Remove from the oven, pick the meat from the bones and allow it to simmer over a low heat in the juices of the oven dish until it is nearly dry.
- Melt a knob of butter in a pan and fry the fillets.
  Allow to bake for another 10 minutes in the oven (150 °C).
  Remove from the pan and keep them warm.
- Deglaze the pan with the rest of the fond and beer and add the sauce.
  Pour through a chinois sieve and mix 30 grammes butter into the mixture.
- Cut the fillets into diagonal slices.

Presentation

- Divide the *confit* of the legs between 4 plates and arrange the fillet slices on top.
- Sprinkle the shrimps on top and drizzle the sauce around it.
- Serve with a delicious potato puree and/or vegetable stew with fresh basil.

Beer Pairing tip

St. Bernardus Pater 6
St. Bernardus Brewery, Watou
Belgian Abbey Ale

Full-bodied flavour.
The perfect marriage between land and sea (The Breton "Armor" means "land by the water") demands the turbulence of this deep dark carbonated drink.

Javanais of duck liver marinated in St. Bernardus Abt 12 with *Kruydekoucke* and Ganda ham

Beer Pairing tip

St. Bernardus Abt 12
St. Bernardus Brewery, Watou
Belgian Abbey Ale

Fruity aroma and soft, full-bodied flavour. The soft velvet froth slowly descends down to the lowest keys of cocoa.

1 kg raw duck liver
(as fresh as possible)
20 g salt
10 cl St. Bernardus Abt 12
slices of Ganda ham
slices of *peperkoek*
(Flemish ginger cake)
a terrine mould

Preparation

- Open the duck liver and remove all the blood vessels.
  Break the lobes into smaller pieces and mix the beer under it.
  Season with salt and pepper, cover with cling film and let the liver stand in the refrigerator overnight.
- Place a layer of liver in the terrine, then slices of Ganda ham, followed by ginger cake. Repeat this until there are 9 layers in total.
- Put the lid on the terrine and leave in a bain-marie in the oven for some 45 minutes at 90 °C.
- Allow the *javanais* to set in the refrigerator overnight and cut into slices.

Beer Pairing tip

Grotten Santé
Kazematten Brewery, Ypres
Local Specialty Beer

Pleasant fruity aroma; strikes the right balance between bitter and sweet. The haze of a mysterious aroma carefully carries this bitter-sweet promise to a climax.

Chocolate ice cream with *sabayon* of Grotten Santé

Preparation

8 egg yolks
8 tbsp Grotten Santé
8 tbsp caster sugar
4 tbsp chocolate ice cream

- Whisk the egg yolks with the beer in a high-sided pan.
- Add the sugar bit by bit, whisking constantly.
- Place the pan on the hob over a low heat and whisk until the sauce begins to thicken.

Presentation

Divide the *sabayon* between 4 glasses
and add to each glass a spoonful of chocolate ice cream.

Panna cotta of dark chocolate with *kletskoppen* (ginger snaps) and Egg nog, served with St. Bernardus Christmas Ale

Panna cotta

3 gelatine sheets
25 cl cream
15 g sugar
25 cl whole milk
125 g dark chocolate
15 g sugar
4 ramekins

- Soak the gelatine sheets in cold water.
- Bring the cream, milk and sugar to the boil, remove from the hob and let the chocolate melt in the mixture.
- Mix the squeezed gelatine sheets in with the chocolate until they are dissolved and divide the mixture between the ramekins.
- Allow to set for several hours.

Kletskoppen (gingersnaps)

25 g butter
75 g brown sugar
35 g flour
baking paper

- Mix the soft butter, sugar and flour well. Add just enough hot water to make the mixture liquid and easier to spread out.
- Scoop a few blobs on a sheet of baking paper and spread out as thinly as possible. Place the *kletskoppen* (ginger snaps) in a pre-heated oven for 8 minutes at 180 °C.
- Allow to cool on the paper.

Egg nog

10 egg yolks (200 g)
20 g vanilla sugar
250 g coffee cream
(concentrated milk)
400 g caster sugar
125 ml Houblonesse

- Whisk the yolks, vanilla sugar and coffee cream to a *sabayon* on the hob.
- Slowly add the sugar. Add the Houblonesse while stirring.
- Pour the egg nog in a jar and leave to cool.

Presentation

- Arrange a number of panna cotta on the plate.
- Insert a *kletskop* (ginger snap) in each of the panna cotta.
- Drizzle some egg nog on the plate and garnish with slivers of candied orange zest if you so wish.

Beer Pairing tip

St. Bernardus Christmas Ale
St. Bernardus Brewery, Watou
Dark Christmas Ale

Malt-fruity, full-bodied taste; the aftertaste is more sweet than bitter. Chocolate and Christmas! Complement each other in an age-old alliance.

The sea is never far away ...

A culinary promise

Inexhaustible source of inspiration, perpetual motion, soothing mantra … the immense water that is at the source of all life on Earth is described, sung and praised to the skies in all manner of ways. Not least as earth mother and generous giver of innumerable delights. Crustaceans, shellfish, fish, octopuses, sea urchins and finned mammals, they have all found their way to the kitchen where, more often than not, have been awarded first prize. That is not surprising, because the alarming pollution notwithstanding, they remain the main suppliers of essential ingredients, such as vitamins, proteins, minerals and unsaturated fatty acids. Occasionally, 't Hommelhof will include a lesser known, or forgotten, species on the menu, because one thing's for sure, our very own North Sea boasts such diversity that you really do not need to go to the other side of the world to serve up something delicious every day. Every week, the chef checks out the local fish market, if only to buy the best piece of cod. Our Belgian shrimp is considered the best in its class, and if you can get them fresh from the fishermen, this is absolutely true. The lobsters from the Oosterschelde effortlessly withstand a round of blind tasting and mussels from Zeeland are second to none the world over.

Fresh fish, whether fried, boiled or steamed, is a real treat, but also the dried varieties make for exquisite results in combination with the expertise of an inspired chef. Most fish are also suitable to be preserved in a spicy acidic solution, and even if this is no longer necessary for the purpose of keeping them for a long period of time, it still is a true delicacy.
Increasingly, we also get the fish served raw. Paper thin slithers that take you back to the salty paradise from whence they came. Who does not fall for a silky *maatjes* herring which is happy to be paired with a chopped onion? Can you get any closer to the sea than when you enjoy a Zeeland oyster? When you take a walk along the beach later on, the sea will never smell the same. You will unwittingly inhale the culinary promise which it has to offer in spades.

Sea bass marinated *à la minute* in Reninge Krieken Rood with samphire, tomato chutney and cream of watercress

Chutney

8 red cherry tomatoes
8 yellow cherry tomatoes
1 tsp pine nuts
1 tsp raisins
1 tsp caster sugar
1 tsp white wine vinegar

- Cut the tomatoes into quarters and add them with the other ingredients in a pot.
- Bring to the boil and simmer for 5 minutes. Leave to cool down.

Cream of watercress

1 bundle of watercress
10 cl sour cream

- Blanch the watercress in boiling salted water and cool in ice water.
- Drain and mix in a blender.
- Add the sour cream. Season with salt and pepper.

Marinade

2 tbsp olive oil
1 tbsp white wine vinegar
2 tbsp Reninge Krieken Rood
coarse salt / pepper

- Mix all ingredients.

Samphire

100 g samphire

- Blanch the samphire briefly in boiling, salted water and cool in ice water.

Presentation

400 g sea bass fillet

- Cut the sea bass into very thin slices (Carpaccio) and arrange them on the plate.
- Brush the marinade on the fish and sprinkle the samphire on top.
- Put a few tufts of chutney on the plate and pipe dots of watercress puree in between.
- Garnish with some more young vegetable shoots, if you so wish.

Beer Pairing tip

Reninge Krieken Rood
Seizoensbrouwerij Vandewalle, Lo-Reninge
Fruity Old Brown

Deep red touches of Veurne sour cherries against a tart backdrop. The complementary flavours meet in a composition with fresh touches.

Salad of tomatoes, *mozzarella di bufala* 'Casa Madaio' and hand-peeled North Sea shrimps served with Oer Beer

Dried tomato

1 kumato tomato

- Peel the kumato tomato, cut it into quarters and remove the seeds.
- Arrange the quarters on an underlay and let them dry for several hours in the oven at 80 °C. Allow to cool.

Ketchup (large quantity)

600 g yellow tomatoes
¼ yellow pepper
¼ onion
½ bay leaf
3 peppercorns
some coriander seeds
1 clove
1 star aniseed
pinch cayenne pepper
pinch of nutmeg
2.5 cl white wine vinegar
35 g caster sugar

- Put all the ingredients in a saucepan, bring to the boil and leave to simmer for 20 minutes.
- Blend the mixture and rub the sauce through a sieve.
- Let the ketchup cool.

Chutney

8 red cherry tomatoes
8 yellow cherry tomatoes
1 tsp pine nuts
1 tsp raisins
1 tsp caster sugar
1 tsp white wine vinegar

- Cut the tomatoes into quarters and leave them to boil with the other ingredients for 5 minutes.

Presentation

2 roma tomatoes
olive oil
coarse salt
200 g hand-peeled shrimps
120 g *mozzarella di bufala*
a few sprigs of basil

- Cut the roma tomatoes very thinly (Carpaccio) and arrange them on a plate so that they overlap.
- Drizzle with olive oil and sprinkle with coarse salt.
- Divide the shrimps and mozzarella between the tomatoes.
- Place a few dried tomatoes in between them and spoon some ketchup and chutney on top. Garnish with shredded basil.

Beer Pairing tip

Oer Beer
De Dolle Brouwers Brewery, Esen
Strong Double

Full-bodied, touches of hop-bitter, malt-bitter, sweet and a little tart. A great deal of character and long aftertaste. The sweet tomato finds its deep strength in the bitter undertones of the Oer Beer. No confrontation, but a firm alliance instead.

Sole fillet with sweetbreads and sea lavender in Reninge Bitter Blond

Preparation the day before

200 g sweetbreads
(of the heart)
carrot/leek/celery/onion
(stock vegetables)
15 cl Reninge Bitter Blond
1 sprig of thyme
1 bay leaf

- Leave the sweetbreads to soak for 2 hours in cold salted water.
- Drain the water and rinse the sweetbreads under the cold water tap.
- Place the sweetbreads in a pan and add water to cover them. Add the bouillon vegetables, the bay leaf, thyme and the beer. Season with salt and pepper. Leave to simmer for 20 minutes.
- Remove the sweetbreads from the stock, peel them and divide them into four portions. Allow to set in the refrigerator.
- Strain the stock and reduce by half.

Preparation on the day

8 sole fillets
flour
50 g (clarified) butter
50 g butter
200 g sea lavender (vegetable)
5 cl peanut oil
shredded chervil

- Fold the sole fillets into three and roll the parcels in the flour. Roll the pieces of sweetbreads in the flour, too.
- Fry the meat and fish in the clarified butter until they are nice and crisp all round.
- Mix 50 grammes of butter in the stock until the liquid is fluffy.
- Pan-fry, just before serving, the rinsed sea lavender in some peanut oil for a very short time.

Presentation

- Scoop some stock in a hot, deep plate and arrange two sole fillets and some sea lavender on top.
- Arrange a piece of sweetbread on the sea lavender and garnish with some shredded chervil.

Beer Pairing tip

Reninge Bitter Blond
Seizoensbrouwerij Vandewalle, Lo-Reninge
Blond, mixed re-fermentation

Pronounced hoppy taste, sharp and bitter. The sweetbreads beautifully reconcile sea and sand.

Flounder filled with fine *brunoise* of vegetables and glazed with Boskeun

4 flounder
flour
1 knob of butter
2 tbsp peanut oil
vegetables of your choice:
carrot, celery, pepper,
courgette, fennel…
3 dl fish stock
10 cl Boskeun
1 dl cream
100 g ice cold butter
2 tbsp whipped cream

Preparation

- Cover the flounder in flour, shake off the excess flour and pan-fry the fish in a knob of hot butter and oil.
- Cut the vegetables into *brunoise* and bring them to the boil briefly in the fumet.
- Strain the vegetables but keep the cooking liquid. Rinse them under the cold water tap.
- Place the cooking liquid and beer on the hob and reduce to half its original volume. Add the cream and reduce by half again.
- Add lumps of cold butter and whisk them into the mixture over a low heat. Add the whipped cream just before serving.
- Carefully bone the fried flounder.

Presentation

- Reconstruct the fish on the plate by placing the fillets on top of each other and inserting the *brunoise* in between the layers.
- Dab the fish with the sauce and place the plate under the grill until golden brown and crispy.

Beer Pairing tip

Boskeun
De Dolle Brouwers Brewery, Esen
Tripel, Easter Beer

Soft with festive bitter touches in a mellow backdrop.
A fish without tricks and a beer without antics. Perfect!

Brill fillet with artichoke, *brandade*, mussels, clams and Single Green Hop

Artichoke puree and watercress butter

4 artichoke hearts
15 cl cream
1 bundle of watercress
50 g butter

- Cook the artichoke hearts for 10 minutes in the cream, puree them in the food processor and season with salt and pepper.
- Blend the watercress with the butter.

Mussels, clams and brill

16 mussels
16 clams
25 cl fish fond
15 cl Single Green Hop
25 cl cream
4 brill fillets (ca. 200 g each)

- Cook the mussels and the clams in the fumet with the beer. Season with salt and pepper.
- Pour the liquid through a sieve and reduce to half its original volume.
- Add the cream and reduce by half again.
- Mix the watercress butter in the sauce.
- Grill the brill fillets on both sides in a hot grill pan and leave them to bake for a further 5 minutes in the oven at 135 °C.

Brandade

200 g cod
10 cl fish fond
2 cloves of garlic
100 g potatoes *annabelle*
40 g butter
16 cl cream

- Cut the cod into pieces and poach in the fish fond with the garlic.
- Boil the potatoes until done, crush them with a fork and add butter and cream.
- Add the cod.
- Season with salt and pepper.

Presentation

- Spoon some brandade on the hot plate and place a brill fillet on top.
- Drizzle the sauce around it.
- Draw a line of artichoke puree and place the mussels and clams on top.

Beer Pairing tip

Single Green Hop
De Plukker Brewery, Poperinge
Blond

Unique and velvety hop flavour thanks to fresh Golding hops. The honest substructure of this pure brew is in perfect harmony with the soft texture of noble fish.

den Overdraght

Each sheep species has its own qualities.

As wealth increases in Belgium, the number of small livestock has dwindled, and so it happened that anyone who wanted a tasty lamb chop was forced to resort to imports from distant lands. Fortunately, some people had the vision to realise that in this way, we are wasting our living heritage, and so Filip and Ann decided to do something about this. In 1995, they took over the family business as a third generation. The farm's main focus at the time was dairy cattle, breeding and fattening pigs, pastures and arable land. In order to attain a better grazing result on the pastures, Filip introduced a flock of sheep, because they eat the grass which dairy cattle will turn their noses up to: the areas around the cowpats. Not only does this save time mowing the grass with the tractor, but as the sheep also eat most weed species, the use of herbicides is reduced to a minimum. Ann, who had completed a dress-making course, saw the potential of those furry friends on four legs, and started using their wool in a creative way. This is how the twin business came about.

Meat and wool

Each sheep species has its own qualities, though. If you breed sheep mainly for the wool, then ideally you would want Devon and Cornwall Longwool, Merino, Gotland fur sheep, Walliser Schwarznase or Flemish sheep.
If you opt for the meat, then you would be better off getting the Ardennes Voskop sheep or the Boulonnais. It is often difficult to choose. What all seven have in common is that they are old varieties, which means that they are quite often threatened with extinction. So den Overdraght ensures that the sheep herd not only remains varied, they also make sure that you get the most delicious piece of lamb on your plate. Animal kindness is, of course, paramount, which means that you not only feed them the best, but that you also ensure that they spend their days as comfortably as possible. Filip and Ann call it their Watch and Do Farm, where you are always welcome for an instructive visit or an activity.

Watch and Do Farm
den Overdraght
Filip en Ann Louwagie-Decrock
Victor-Louise-Ernest
Woestenseweg 31
8970 Poperinge, Belgium
Tel./Fax: +32 (0)57 33 31 09
www.denoverdraght.be

Shoulder of lamb braised in honey and Keikop Blond with hop shoots and mashed sweet potato

800 g boneless shoulder of lamb tied in a roulade
1 onion
1 carrot
1 stalk of green celery
1 sprig of rosemary
20 g honey
10 cl Keikop Blond
25 cl brown fond
6 large sweet potatoes
200 g hop shoots
½ lemon
25 cl cream
nutmeg
20 g butter

Preparation

- Pre-heat the oven at 100 °C.
- Season the meat with salt and pepper and char in some browned butter. Add the coarsely cut onion, carrot, celery and rosemary and allow them to stew for a while.
- Baste the browned shoulder of lamb with honey. Pour over the beer and the brown fond.
- Cover the meat with aluminium foil and bring to the boil. Leave it to simmer for 6 to 7 hours in a pre-heated oven at 100°C.
- Peel the sweet potatoes, cut into chunks and boil them in salted water. Drain them, let them dry out on a low heat and puree them. Season with pepper, salt and a knob of butter.
- Wash the hop shoots thoroughly in vinegar water and boil them in salted water with the lemon. Remove from the hob as soon as they have reached boiling point and drain. If you boil them in advance, allow them to cool in the cooking liquid.
- Reduce the cream with a pinch of salt, pepper and nutmeg to half its original volume. Heat the hop shoots in this mixture.

Presentation

- Place a scoop of mashed potato on the plate and arrange the meat on top.
- Dress with the reduced gravy of the meat and cover with some hop shoots.

Beer Pairing tip

Keikop Blond
De Plukker Brewery, Poperinge
Dark Blond

Complex hoppyness that is in harmony with the malts used. The deep accents of the braised meat dissolve slowly in the dark blond nectar.

Blanquette of lamb tongue with Arabier

12 lamb tongues
1 carrot
1 stalk of green celery
1 onion
2 turnips
½ broccoli
spring-onion
thyme and bay leaf
1 tbsp tomato puree
25 cl Arabier
25 cl cream
2 hard-boiled eggs
4 pickled gherkins

Preparation

- Leave the tongues to soak overnight in cold, salted water and rinse well.
- Bring to the boil in cold, salted water.
  Add the finely chopped vegetables (except the broccoli), thyme and bay leaf as soon as the water boils.
  Allow the tongues with the vegetables to simmer for 15 minutes.
- Remove the tongues from the bouillon, peel them and halve them lengthwise.
- Strain the cooking liquid but keep the vegetables to one side.
  Reduce 25 cl with the beer and the tomato puree to half the original volume.
  Add the cream and reduce by half again.
- Poach the broccoli florets.
- Mash the eggs and slice the gherkins.
- Heat the cooked vegetables with the tongues in the rest of the stock.

Presentation

- Place 6 half tongues on a hot plate in a fan shape.
- Scoop some sauce over it and finish off with the cooked vegetables.
- Scatter some gherkins on top.

Serving suggestion

A fluffy potato mousseline is equally delicious with this recipe.

Beer Pairing tip

Arabier
De Dolle Brouwers, Esen
Strong Blond

The Poperinge nugget hop bells, somewhat held in check by the pale malt, add a kick of bitterness at the end. The special texture of the soft meat is set off against the firm, fiery tartness.

Beer Pairing tip

Kapittel Prior
Van Eecke Brewery, Watou
Abbey Beer

Full-bodied and firm with an impressive range of fragrances, including alcohol, chocolate, spices, slightly roasted malts. Slightly bitter aftertaste with a sweet finish.

Lamb in Kapittel Prior with ragu of spring vegetables

4 young carrots
4 spring onions
4 turnips
4 green asparagus
4 white asparagus
80 g peas
80 g mangetout
100 g butter
1 tsp caster sugar
800 g boneless leg of lamb
1 l brown fond
10 cl Kapittel Prior
1 tsp yellow mustard seed

Preparation

- Preheat the oven to 180 °C.
- Wash all the vegetables and cut them into chunks.
- Blanch the green vegetables briefly and cool them down in ice water to retain their fresh colour.
- Put the carrots, turnips, spring onions and white asparagus into a pot with a little water. Add a knob of butter, salt and pepper, and sugar, place the lid on the pot and bring to the boil.
  Add the blanched vegetables and leave to cook for 10 minutes under the lid.
- Season the meat with salt and pepper and brown all around in butter.
- Place the meat in an oven dish and leave to bake in the oven for some 10 minutes (depending on the thickness).
- Deglaze the pan with the beer and the fond, add mustard seeds and reduce to a sauce-like consistency.

Presentation

- Form with a quarter of the vegetables a rectangular bed on a warm plate and place 1 asparagus on top.
- Arrange some slices of the meat on the vegetables so that they overlap, and spoon some sauce over it.

The *fine fleur* of vegetables

De Lovie

Here, you rediscover the taste of Jerusalem artichoke and parsnip.

If you look for small-scale farmers or breeders, you automatically end up in family businesses: well-kept secrets that are handed down from father to son with elbow grease as the main source of energy. At De Lovie, this is slightly different. The estate was built by Jules van Merris 200 years ago as a summer residence. Even though the neoclassical castle with farm buildings and a vast English garden still evoke the grandeur of a bygone era, the site was given a new purpose in the 1960s.
Today, De Lovie is a centre that offers quality support to people with a mental handicap, and centres its activities around the farm buildings. Under the watchful eye of carers with expertise in agricultural and horticultural techniques, a number of residents are given the opportunity to demonstrate their green skills.

There is no pressure to do well, and so everything is done at the gentle pace of nature. To make a difference, we particularly plant 'forgotten' vegetables. Growing these is very labour-intensive, but the level of satisfaction is proportionate. The range of plants on offer is reminiscent of a travel guide to an exotic destination, but each one of them are local produce which were found in many allotments in days gone by. Potatoes are not just called *Bintje* but also *Ratte, Anabelle, Corne de gatte, Vitelotte* and *Gourmandine*. This is where you rediscover the taste of Jerusalem artichoke, *Crosnes* (tubers of the Japanese knotroot) and parsnips. All products are harvested manually, and subsequently cleaned and packaged with the utmost care. They are marketed with the 'Flandria' and 'Fine Fleur' label, a guarantee that the product is fresh and meets stringent quality standards.
These delicacies are sold at spot prices. De Lovie also makes it a point of honour to be the first to offer hop shoots at the *Reo Veiling* (Agricultural Auction Market), something the residents are very proud of.

De Lovie
Krombeekseweg
8970 Poperinge, Belgium
Tel: +32 (0)57 33 83 26
www.delovie.be

EXP
LOS
IVE

Salad of potato, herring fillet, parsnip, apple cream with Antique Blond Super Ale 5

Beer Pairing tip

Antique Blond Super Ale 5
Deca Brewery, Woesten
Ale

Pared down simplicity contrasting with a tangy undertone of lightly salted quark and tingling bubbles.

Preparation the day before

3 Jonagold apples
50 g demerara sugar
25 cl Antique Blond Super Ale 5
1 *ratte* potato
1 *corne de gatte*
1 *vitelotte* (truffle potato)
1 parsnip
10 cl cream
10 g butter
4 pickled herring fillets
20 dandelion salad leaves

- Peel and core the apples, cut them into pieces and cook them in the sugar for 10 minutes.
- Reduce the beer to one quarter, mix it with the apple sauce and whisk until you obtain a cream-like consistency.
- Cook the 3 potatoes in their skins in salted water.
- Peel the parsnip and slice 16 wafer thin slivers using the slicer. Fry the parsnip slices at 140 °C until crisp. Leave to drain on kitchen towel.
- Cut the rest of the parsnip into pieces and boil them in salted water until they are done. Whisk the soft parsnip with the cream to a smooth consistency and stir the butter in it.
- Peel the potatoes and cut them into disks.
- Wash and dry the dandelion salad.

Presentation

- Divide the potato disks, parsnip crisps and herring fillets between the plates.
- Add tufts of apple and parsnip cream and garnish with dandelion salad.

Carpaccio of tomato, sour cream with oxtail and beef *consommé* with Ypres AKA Wipers

Bouillon and oxtail

4 large carrots
4 leeks
6 stalks of white celery
4 onions
4 cloves of garlic
a few sprigs of thyme
1 bundle of parsley stems
4 bay leaves
2 sprigs of rosemary
1 tbsp black peppercorns
2 cloves
25 cl Ypres AKA Wipers
1 oxtail (in pieces)

- Cut the washed leek, carrots, celery and onion into chunks and put them in a large pot. Add the crushed garlic cloves.
  Tie the thyme, rosemary, bay leaves and parsley stems into a *bouquet garni* and add to the vegetables. Crush the peppercorns and cloves in a mortar and scatter them over the vegetables.
- Submerge the vegetables, add the beer and oxtail and bring to the boil over a low heat.
- Leave the stock to simmer for 4 hours, with lid, until the meat falls off the bone.
- Scoop the pieces of tail from the stock and leave them to cool down.
- Pour the stock through a sieve and bring to the boil over a medium heat.

Finish

6 egg whites
200 g minced beef
1 tin tomato puree (70 g)
1 large carrot
cayenne pepper
4 tbsp sour cream
2 roma tomatoes
1 tbsp olive oil
coarse salt
shredded chervil

- Place the egg whites, the ground beef and the tomato puree in a blender and season with salt and pepper (there is no salt yet in the stock).
  Blend the ingredients until you obtain a *clarif*.
- Decant the *clarif* into the cooking stock and whisk immediately.
  Leave the stock to simmer for some 20 minutes over a medium heat.
- In the mean time, cut the peeled carrot into fine *brunoise*, blanch it briefly and leave to cool down.
- Scoop the coagulated protein cake from the bouillon and pour the *consommé* through a sieve with a piece of muslin.
- Pick the meat from the oxtail and pull it into threads.
  Collect the fine meat threads in a bowl.
- Bring the clarified *consommé* gently to the boil.
- Season the sour cream with pepper and cayenne pepper and scoop a spoonful through the cooled *brunoise*.

Presentation

- Cut the tomatoes into very thin slices, arrange them on a deep plate and drizzle some olive oil over them. Season with pepper and coarse salt.
- Heat the meat in some *consommé* and divide between the plates.
- Place a dollop of sour cream on the meat and cover with the carrots.
- Serve the hot *consommé* at the table and pour over the dish.
- Finish off with some shredded chervil.

Beer Pairing tip

Ypres AKA Wipers
Struise Brouwers Brewery, Oostvleteren
Flemish Old Brown

The sweetness of the beer goes hand in hand with the soft sunlight of the tomato. The fresh lactic acid complements the clear *consommé* but appropriately contrasts with the meat.

Veal ragu, young vegetables and watercress with Antique Blond 8, penne scented with orange

850 g veal ragu
25 g butter
½ l pale veal fond
½ bottle Antique Blond 8
1 sprig of sage
1 sprig of thyme
5 sprigs of fresh coriander
young vegetables:
carrot, turnip, spring onion, ...
1 unsprayed orange
500 g penne
75 g butter
2 tbsp cream

Preparation

- Gently brown the veal in some butter and quench with the fond and the beer. Add the herbs and leave the meat to simmer until it is completely cooked.
- Add the finely chopped young vegetables.
- Zest the orange.
- Cook the penne in salted water.
- Melt the butter with the juice of the orange and reduce until it has a syrup-like consistency.
  Add the zest and add the cooked penne to heat it up.
- Spoon the cream through the veal ragu just before serving.

Presentation

- Place the veal with the vegetables in a deep plate.
- Arrange the penne with sauce around it and garnish with a few fresh herbs.

Beer Pairing tip

Antique Blond 8
Deca Brewery, Woesten
Ale

Full-bodied in character, slightly bitter. The frivolity of a mad spring is slightly dampened by the subtle bitterness of a full ale.

Holstein sirloin in Snoek Bruin with beetroot, crumble of onion, marrow, green beans and autumn truffle

Crumble

¼ onion
25 g butter
50 g breadcrumbs made from stale bread

- Sauté the chopped onion in the butter and add the breadcrumbs.
- Allow the mixture to dry for 20 minutes in the oven at 180 °C.

Beetroot and marrowbones

1 beetroot
1 tbsp honey
2 marrowbones

- Boil the beetroot for 45 minutes in salted water. Drain, peel the beetroot and cut it into small cubes. Just before serving, rub them in warm honey.
- Boil the marrowbones in salted water for 15 minutes. Remove the marrow and leave to cool. Cut the set marrow into slices.

Sirloin and green beans

4 x 200 g Holstein sirloin
10 g butter
15 cl Snoek Bruin
20 cl brown fond
100 g green beans
nutmeg

- Char the meat on both sides in the hot butter.
- Bake it for 5 minutes in the oven at 180 °C. Remove the meat from the pan and let it rest for 10 minutes.
- Deglaze the pan with the beer and the fond, strain and reduce to sauce thickness.
- Cut the beans into thin strips and fry them in the melted butter. Season with salt and pepper and a little nutmeg.

Presentation

- Heat the marrow slices in the sauce.
- Arrange the green beans and beetroot on the plate and place the meat and vegetables on top.
- Spoon some sauce over it and sprinkle with the crumble.
- Add another slice of marrow on top and possibly some truffle shavings.

Beer Pairing tip

Snoek Bruin
Malt and brewery house De Snoek, Alveringem
Dark Ale

The warm sensation of a dark beer frames like no other the tough finesse of excellent beef.

Liquid gold

Het Sas & Van Eecke

Well-kept secrets ...

With a quality product like Hommel Beer as part of the range, the presumption that the brewery that sells this traditional product is not just any brewery is correct. From Carolus Leroy to Hendrik & Filip Leroy, we counted no fewer than seven generations of brewing talent under one roof, whilst the site housed brewing activities back in the second half of the 17th century, or so we believe. If this is true, this makes it the oldest brewery in the country. And every generation has added something, of course. First, there was a merger, which ensured that both capacity and craftsmanship doubled.
When well-kept secrets are pitted against each other … 'du choc des idées jaillit la lumière' [from a clash of ideas comes light]! Today's challenge is, more than ever, about commercialising the product, and in order to do this, it is paramount we acquire a pole position on the digital highway. Consequently, the media specialist became just as much a fixture in the company as the brewer, even though craftsmanship remains the alfa and omega of the noble art of brewing, of course.
Never before has the range of beers been so extensive, never before has the choice been so difficult.

With their 15 beers, the breweries do not immediately provide a solution to that problem, but nobody's complaining. Now that it is becoming increasingly clear that beer, enjoyed within reason, is a blessing for life and limb, you can skip the odd doctor's visit thanks to the better beer brewer. Each brew is good for something, but they all stimulate the same degree of good mood. The latter is probably largely due to the use of real Poperinge hops, which, like no other, succeed in extracting the subtlety of liquid gold. Meanwhile, the eighth generation is champing at the bit to get started, which means the future of Het Sas and Van Eecke is safe.

Het Sas Brewery
Diksmuidseweg 406
8904 Boezinge, Belgium
Tel: +32 (0)57 42 20 05
www.brouwerijhetsas.be

Van Eecke Brewery
Douvieweg 2
8978 Watou, Belgium
Tel: +32 (0)57 38 80 30
www.brouwerijvaneecke.be

poperings
hommel
bier
poperings
hommel
bier
poperings
hommel
bier
QKF-380
60
PACTON
A&D

PALM
HET KAPITTEL
WATOU

Salmon rillettes with Ridder, *coulis* of cauliflower and broccoli florets

Preparation

200 g chunks of salmon fillet
25 cl olive oil
25 cl Ridder
20 g chopped dill
¼ cauliflower
5 cl cream
12 thin toast
sprigs of dill

- Cook salmon chunks for 15 minutes in the oil and beer.
  Keep stirring while the beer evaporates.
- Season with salt and pepper, put the salmon and oil in a bowl and add the chopped dill.
  Stir the rillettes well and allow them to cool for at least 2 hours.
- Keeping a few florets to one side, cook the rest of the cauliflower in salted water until very tender. Place the soft cauliflower in the blender and blend with the cream. Season the coulis with salt and pepper.
- Blanch the broccoli florets in boiling, salted water and subsequently rinse them in ice water.

Presentation

- Make 3 puddles of coulis on the plates and arrange one dollop of rillettes on top of each one.
- Arrange the broccoli florets around them, garnish with a sprig of dill and insert a thin piece of toast into each dollop.

Beer Pairing tip

Ridder
Van Eecke Brewery, Watou
Low-alcohol

low-alcohol thirst quencher. Fresh, fragrant and slightly bitter. Extra shine thanks to a modest entourage. Ridder [knight] at the emperor's service.

Carpaccio of cod marinated in Katje with sour cream

400 g cod fillet
(skinless)
10 cl olive oil
10 cl fish fumet
10 cl Katje
1 young carrot
1 celery stalk
½ leek
100 g sour cream
1 pinch cayenne pepper
mix of fresh garden herbs
(chives, dill, coriander, chervil…)
a few pink peppercorns
bread crusts fried in peanut oil

Preparation

- Wrap the cod fillet in plastic film and let it rest in the freezer for a few hours.
- For the marinade, bring the olive oil, fish fumet and the beer to the boil, together with the finely chopped vegetables.
- Season the sour cream with salt, pepper and cayenne pepper and divide it between 4 dinner plates.
- Cut with a meat slicer the cod in 2mm thin slices and arrange these on the cream. Coat with the marinade, using a little brush, and place the marinated vegetables on top.
- Season the fish and place the plates for another minute in a pre-heated oven at 180 °C allowing the fish to flake.

Presentation

Finish off the plates with finely chopped garden herbs, pink peppercorns and bread crusts.

Beer Pairing tip

Katje Special
Van Eecke Brewery, Watou
Dark Ale

Complete but punchy. Slightly sweet with prominent malt aroma. Very thin finesse cooked on a dark cloud of purified passion.

Gazpacho of green asparagus and SAS Lager with panna cotta of Ganda ham and white asparagus

Gazpacho

1 bundle of green asparagus
10 cl SAS lager
50 cl chicken fond

- Remove the tough ends of the green asparagus.
- Boil 4 green asparagus for 5 minutes until *al dente*. These will be used to garnish.
- Cut up the rest of the green asparagus, blanch and cool in ice water. Simmer them for 20 minutes in the beer and fond, season with salt and pepper. Blend the mixture and rub through a chinois sieve.
- Allow the soup to rest overnight in the refrigerator.

Panna cotta

1 bundle of white asparagus
8 gelatine sheets
2 slices of Ganda ham
25 cl double cream
12 equal moulds

- Carefully peel the white asparagus and remove the hard ends.
- Boil 4 green asparagus for 5 minutes until *al dente*. These will be used to garnish.
- Boil the rest of the asparagus for 20 minutes in lightly salted water. Five minutes before the end of the cooking time, soak the gelatine sheets in water.
- Blend the cooked asparagus and add the squeezed gelatine sheets and pepper. Fold the finely chopped ham (which provides the salt) and the cream under the the mixture and pour into the moulds.
- Leave the panna cotta to rest overnight in the refrigerator.

Presentation

- Scoop some soup in the chilled plates, and place the panna cotta on top.
- Arrange 1 green and 1 white asparagus on top.

Beer Pairing tip

SAS Lager
Van Eecke Brewery, Watou
Lager Beer

Malty aroma with a bitter aftertaste. The modest input of an honest lager lifts the grandeur of noble products to another plane and is therefore entitled to some of the credit.

Homemade *sauerkraut* with *escabeche* of mackerel in Sasbrau

Sauerkraut

¼ white cabbage
25 cl white wine vinegar
25 cl white wine Monteberg
1 tsp caster sugar
1 level tbsp of coarse salt

- Clean the cabbage: cut it into quarters, loosen the leaves, remove the core and the large veins.
  Cut the cabbage leaves into thin strips.
- Bring the vinegar, white wine, sugar and coarse salt to the boil and pour the mixture on the chopped cabbage.
  Mix well, cover with cling film and leave to marinate for one day.

Escabeche

4 mackerel fillets (with skin)
1 small carrot
1 leek (white only)
1 stalk of green celery
2 spring onions
25 cl Sasbrau
10 cl white wine vinegar
1 bundle of dill
4 tbsp sour cream
cayenne pepper

- Arrange the mackerel fillets, skin side up, next to each other in a shallow dish.
- Finely cut the vegetables and bring them to the boil in the beer and vinegar.
  As soon as the liquid has reached boiling point, remove from the hob and pour over the fish.
  Cover the dish with plastic foil and leave to cool.
- Mix the sour cream with the chopped dill, salt and cayenne pepper.
  Keep a few sprigs of dill for garnish later.

Presentation

- Place some *sauerkraut* in the centre of the plate and divide the marinated vegetables between the plates.
- Arrange a piece of fish on the vegetables.
- Spoon a few dots of sour cream around the dish.
- Garnish with sprigs of dill.

Beer Pairing tip

Sasbrau
Van Eecke Brewery, Watou
Dortmunder Lager

Sturdy and aromatic.
Strong malt and hop aroma.
Fermented suppleness where the fish reconciles two champions.

Bavarois of smoked *Oosterschelde* eel with espuma of dandelion salad and Watou's Wit jelly

Bavarois

300 g fillets of smoked *Oosterschelde* eel
150 cl fish fumet
3 sheets of gelatine
150 cl double cream
pinch cayenne pepper

- Poach the eel for 3 minutes in the fish fumet and pour everything into the blender.
- Add during blending the soaked and squeezed gelatine sheets.
- Allow to cool to room temperature.
- Carefully fold the semi-whipped cream under the mixture and check the seasoning.
  Season with salt and pepper to taste but bear in mind that the eel is already salted.
- Pour the bavarois into moulds of your choice.

Espuma

1 head of dandelion salad (wild dandelion)
20 cl double cream
1 sheet of gelatine
espuma bottle with gas cartridge

- Remove the leaves of the dandelion salad, wash and cut into strips. Keep a few leaves back for garnish.
- Cook the strips of dandelion salad for 3 minutes in the cream and stir in the soaked and squeezed gelatine.
- Rub the liquid through a fine sieve.
- Pour the liquid into an espuma bottle and leave to cool in the refrigerator.

Jelly

10 cl Watou's Wit
10 cl *consommé* of fish
2 sheets of gelatine

- Bring the beer with the *consommé* to the boil and season with salt and pepper to taste.
- Dissolve the soaked and squeezed gelatine in the liquid.
- Pour the liquid into a shallow dish and leave to set in the refrigerator.
- Cut up the jelly just before serving.

Presentation

8 poached asparagus tips
100 g poached samphire
100 g peeled shrimps

- Arrange 3 pieces of *bavarois* on a chilled plate and pipe each time a dollop of espuma on top.
- Arrange the jelly sticks, leaves of dandelion salad, samphire, 2 asparagus tips and a few pieces of smoked eel on the plate and sprinkle some shrimps over it.

Beer Pairing tip

Watou's Wit
Van Eecke Brewery, Watou
White Beer

Fresh thirst quencher. Slightly tart in taste with fruity coriander.
A daring split where the acidity of the beer appears to momentarily slow down the velvet texture of the fish to then subsequently dissolve it in a spectacular fashion.

Stew of wild mushrooms in a vegetable stock with Kapittel Blond and goat's cheese sorbet

Bouillon

1 leek
2 carrots
1 onion
1 stalk of green celery
2 bay leaves
1 tsp *fleur de sel*
1 tsp peppercorns
1.5 l water
10 cl Kapittel Blond

- Cut the vegetables into pieces, put them in a pan with the herbs, and add water and beer.
- Cook for 30 minutes.
- Pass through a sieve and keep the liquid warm.

Sorbet

1 egg yolk
80 g caster sugar
70 g very fresh goat's cheese
1 finely chopped clove of garlic
30 cl whole milk
20 cl whipped cream

- Beat the egg yolk and sugar until fluffy.
- Add the goat's cheese with the garlic and some milk. Mix well. Add the rest of the milk.
- Fold with a whisk the cheese mixture under the egg yolk, little by little, and mix well.
- Beat the whipped cream until stiff and carefully fold the cheese mixture under the cream.
- Pour the mixture into the *sorbetière* to make sorbet.

Wild mushrooms

400 g wild mushrooms
25 g butter
1 crushed clove of garlic

- Brown the butter.
- Add the mushrooms and the garlic and allow them to brown in the hot butter. Season with salt and pepper.

Presentation

- Spoon the mushrooms into a warm, deep plate and pour over the boiling bouillon.
- Add, just before serving, a dollop of sorbet to the stock.
- Scatter finely-chopped chives on the plate.

Beer Pairing tip

Kapittel Blond
Van Eecke Brewery, Watou
Abbey Beer

Thirst quencher. Sweet, slight malt aroma. Mysterious stories. Woodland and beech leaves. Heaven and earth: bliss.

Rillettes of tame rabbit scented with SAS Lager

500 g fat/lard
1 onion
1 sprig of thyme
1 bay leaf
1 kg boneless rabbit meat
2 bottles of SAS Lager
a salad of fresh herbs and vegetables
cornet bread or toast

Preparation

- Melt the lard with the finely chopped onion and herbs.
- Cut the meat into fairly large chunks and add to the lard as soon as it starts to bubble.
- Add the beer and bring to the boil.
  Cook the meat for 3 hours over a low heat, stirring vigorously occasionally.
  The meat will go stringy and gradually absorb the taste of the beer (which is reduced).
- Remove the pot from the hob and allow the rillettes to cool down, still stirring occasionally.
  Put them in a china bowl and allow them to set in the refrigerator.

Presentation

Use 2 spoons to make dollops of the rillettes and present them on a plate with a salad and a cornet bread.

Sas Lager
Van Eecke Brewery, Watou
Lager

Powerful, refreshing. Malty aroma with bitter aftertaste. The dead-honest lager accentuates the simple character of a product without pretence.

Beer Pairing tip

Trifle of pomegranate with Yperman

4 pomegranates
200 g strawberries
200 g sugar
10 cl Yperman
2 eggs
1 packet of vanilla sugar
250 g mascarpone
½ lime
6 speculoos biscuits

Preparation

- Deseed the pomegranate and keep 4 tea spoons of the seeds to one side for the garnish.
- Cut the strawberries into pieces, put them in a pan, sprinkle with the sugar and cook until the sugar has dissolved.
  Add the pomegranate seeds and leave to cool.
- Reduce the Yperman to a syrup-like consistency and leave to cool.
  Beat the egg yolks and the sugar to thick consistency and fold the beer syrup under the mixture.
  Mix the mascarpone and lime juice in with the mixture.
- Crumble the speculoos biscuits.

Presentation

- Put a layer of fruit with syrup and a layer of mascarpone in a glass.
- Garnish with pomegranate seeds and crumbled speculoos biscuits.

Beer Pairing tip

Yperman
Van Eecke Brewery, Watou
Ale

Full-bodied. Slightly smoked grain flavour. The soft exotic flair of the pomegranate gives the hint of smouldering wood chips an extra dimension.

Gratin of fresh fruit with *sabayon* of Christmas Leroy and pistachio ice cream

Preparation

4 egg yolks
4 tbsp Christmas Leroy
4 tbsp sugar
fruit salad of fresh seasonal fruit
4 scoops of pistachio ice cream

- Whisk the egg yolks with the beer in a tall saucepan over a low heat.
- Gradually add the sugar while whisking constantly until the mixture has attained a homogenous consistency.

Presentation

- Arrange the fresh fruit salad against the edge of a deep plate and place a scoop of ice cream in the middle of the circle.
- Pour the *sabayon* over the fruit salad and place the plates under the grill until the *sabayon* is slightly discoloured.

Beer Pairing tip

Christmas Leroy
Van Eecke Brewery, Watou
Special Beer, winter beer

Pronounced spicy touch: liquorice, cherry and Curacao.

De Beauvoordse Walhoeve

They are not worried about the quality of the milk.

Veurne-Ambacht, you will not find anywhere much flatter or greener than here. Endless meadows, vast fields with the occasional line of trees that are unanimous in their leaning to the east. Because the wind is there ... always and everywhere. This is grazing land *par excellence*, and as the enterprising locals have cottoned on to this, they can benefit from it greatly. You start with a herd of Hollstein cattle, you leave them to munch the tender grass to their heart's content and you empty their bursting udders from time to time. Before you know it, you are up to your knees in milk and the question then arises: what now? You can, of course, sell it to the big producers, but then you become one of many. Which is a bit of a shame for a product of the highest quality. The Deeren family decided to process the priceless commodity themselves, and 160 cows later, they can proudly fill a comprehensive display cabinet with all the dairy produce they make on the spot. They are not worried about the quality of the milk, because the farmer takes care of the feed himself! More than half their diet consists of grass, and that is the secret of delicious dairy. That, along with a thorough knowledge of cheese-making, a chunky portion of experience, a professional workshop, together with a boundless love for the job, are the best guarantees for a product that you cannot find anywhere else.

The secret of delicious dairy

Everything began with *'t Zandeke Jong*. This small, flat cheese ball is particularly popular with children on account of its mild flavour. This was quickly followed by the *Blanche*, another while-mould cheese and *De Bryarde*, a punchy cheese with character, matured in beer. *De Wulveringemsche Abt* is a typical monk's cheese: a delightful snack and great with beer. But we could not miss out a farmstead Gouda-type cheese: large balls of young cheese, young mature, mature, old or overdue.

Different herb varieties make the range even more tempting: farmstead cheese with nuts, peppers, tomatoes, garden herbs or mustard seeds ... plenty of choice!

And finally, there are the yoghurts or curds, traditional ice-creams and other puddings.

De Beauvoordse Walhoeve
Fam. J. Deeren-Dequeecker
Vaartstraat 71
8630 Veurne, Belgium
Tel: +32 (0)58 31 16 75
www.beauvoordse-walhoeve.be

WALHOEVE

Poperinge *standevlees* marinated in Westvleteren 8 with pickles and extra mature farmhouse cheese

Preparation the day before

400 g *standevlees*
(pickled and smoked pork loin)
25 cl Westvleteren 8
100 g shavings of extra mature farmhouse cheese

- Put the meat and the beer in a plastic bag and push out the air. Let it steam for 2 hours at 67 °C. Place the wrapped meat immediately in an ice bath and allow to rest that way in the refrigerator overnight.

Pickles

¼ cauliflower
¼ broccoli
1 young carrot
33 cl Westvleteren 8
1 dl white wine vinegar
12 gherkins
20 silverskin onions
1 tbsp mustard seeds
1 bay leaf
1 tbsp curry powder
1 sprig of thyme

- Cut the cauliflower and broccoli into small florets. Cut the carrot into thin slices.
- Bring the beer and white wine vinegar to the boil and add the vegetables. Add after 5 minutes the finely chopped gherkins and silverskin onions. Mix in the curry, bay leaf, thyme and mustard seeds and allow to cook for another 1 minute.
- Put the pickles in jars and leave them to cool down in the refrigerator.

Presentation

- Cut the meat into thin slices and arrange on the plate.
- Brush some juice of the pickles on the meat and arrange some pickles next to it.
- Sprinkle cheese shavings over the plate.
- Garnish with a few sprigs of frisee lettuce.

Beer Pairing tip

Westvleteren 8
Sint-Sixtus Brewery, Westvleteren
Trappist Dark

Sweet, fruity aroma with a melon accent.
The smoky salt comes into its own in the fruity accent of an extremely solid Trappist.

Rabbit back with *'t Zandeke Jong*, spinach and sundried tomato in Snoek Blond, langoustines in their gravy

Beer Pairing tip

Preparation

2 rabbit backs of the Flemish Giant breed
100 g butter
½ bottle Snoek Blond
25 cl brown fond
1 small celeriac
½ lemon
nutmeg
25 g cold butter
12 fresh langoustines
250 g baby spinach
2 slices Watou cheese
some sundried tomatoes
some prunes
12 rocket leaves

- Fillet the rabbit backs, but make sure that the peritoneum is left on the fillets.
- Chop the carcases into pieces, brown them in a pan with some butter and moisten them with the beer and the brown fond.
  Leave the sauce to simmer for 20 minutes.
- Peel the celeriac, cut into chunks and cook for 15 minutes in cold salted water with the lemon.
  Drain the celeriac, allow to dry and puree.
  Season with some salt, pepper and nutmeg.
  Add butter to the puree to bind it and make it shiny.
- Peel the langoustines and make a light *bisque* (see p. 40) with the heads and shells intact.
- Blanch the spinach.
- Lay the rabbit fillets flat and cover the belly flaps with half a slice of Watou cheese, blanched spinach and fine strips of dried tomatoes.
  Roll up the fillets and tie them with kitchen string.
- Melt a knob of butter in a pan over a low heat and brown the roulades in the hazelnut butter. Allow them to bake for another 10 minutes in a fan-assisted oven at 140 °C.
- Pour the beer sauce through a sieve, add the prunes and reduce.
- Mix the cold butter in the *bisque*.
- Remove the roulades from the oven and remove the string.
  Cut them into 2 equal parts.
- Pan-fry the langoustines briefly on both sides in a knob of butter.

Snoek Blond
Malt and brewery house De Snoek, Alveringem
Blond high fermentation

Barley malt and Poperinge hops.
A modern twist on a classic dish: rabbit with prunes.
A natural choice of beer, recognisable ingredients.

Presentation

- Place 3 slices of rabbit meat on one side of the plate and 3 dots of celeriac puree with a langoustine placed on top on the other.
- Drizzle the sauce and the *bisque* in between.
- Garnish the langoustines with a leaf of rocket.

Beer Pairing tip

Orloff of pork stew meat, Duroc d'olives with semi-mature farmhouse cheese in Rookop Dubbel

Preparation

600 g piece of pork stew meat
200 g of sliced farmhouse cheese
1 kg baby spinach
25 g butter
1 red pepper
1 yellow pepper
1 green pepper
½ courgette
½ aubergine
15 cl Rookop Dubbel
20 cl brown fond
1 tbsp peanut oil

- Cut the piece of pork stew meat lengthwise in half, but do not cut all the way through.
  Cut each half further open until you have a large piece of meat.
- Pound the meat flat with a meat mallet and cover with cheese and cooked spinach.
- Roll up the meat into a roulade and wrap in cling film.
  Tighten the roulade well and steam for 45 minutes at 80 °C.
  Allow to rest overnight.
- Melt the butter, remove the roulade from the foil and brown on all sides in the brown butter. Remove the meat from the pan (do not wash the pan yet!) and leave to bake for another 15 minutes in the oven at 130 °C.
- Cut the peppers, courgette and aubergine in *brunoise*.
- Deglaze the pan with the beer and the brown fond and reduce the gravy until it has reached a sauce-like consistency.
- Sauté the *brunoise* in the peanut oil and season with salt and pepper.
- Remove the roulade from the oven and cut into thick slices.

Presentation

- Arrange a line of vegetable *brunoise* on the plate and place 3 slices of roulade on top.
- Spoon the sauce over the dish.

Rookop Double
De Plukker Brewery, Poperinge
Flemish Old Brown

Creamy start with dark chocolate touches.
The soft creamy sensation supports the warmth of creamy cheese and marbled meat.

Soup of red fruit with Struise Witte. Curd yoghurt and lavender sorbet

Preparation the day before

½ l full-fat yoghurt

- Hang a sieve in a bowl, drape a damp muslin cloth over it and pour the full-fat yoghurt into it.
- Leave the yoghurt to drain overnight.

On the day

For the sorbet
½ l sparkling wine
½ l sugar syrup (bring ¼ l water + ¼ kg sugar to the boil)
2 tbsp lavender flowers
or 1 tsp lavender extract
5 cl hopsakei gin
5 cl Struise Witte

1 vanilla pod
1 tbsp honey
100 g raspberries
100 g strawberries
100 g blackberries
100 g blueberries
100 g red berries
4 tbsp sugar
15 cl Struise Witte
15cl hopsakei gin

- Mix the ingredients for the sorbet, pour the mixture into the ice cream machine and switch on, following the instructions. The sorbet has to be creamy in consistency.
- Scoop the curd (drained yoghurt) into a mixing bowl and stir in the honey and the vanilla seeds.
- Put the fruits into a bowl, sprinkle with sugar and add the beer and gin. Leave to infuse for half an hour.

Presentation

- Spoon some fruits with juice into a deep plate, place a scoop of sorbet in the centre and pipe a few tufts of curd around it.
- Garnish with some crumble or a sprig of mint.

Beer Pairing tip

Struise Witte
De Struise Brouwers Brewery, Oostvleteren
White Beer

Refreshing duel between sour and bitter, carried by wheat, citrus and coriander.

Wanted game

Time to dig up the game recipes

In the autumn, forest and field are united on the hob with wonderful creations as a result.

As soon as the mist hangs low over the fields, and only the balding tree tops of the woods become visible, it is time to dust off the game recipes. Thanks to effective nature management, wildlife is greater in numbers than ever before. Roebuck, which avoided this region for years, is being spotted again regularly. Pheasants, hares and rabbits are thriving and when you walk along the barren fields, you may be taken by surprise by an unsuspecting flock of pheasants taking off. Logs are being brought in, woolly sweaters dug up. The shorter days smell of apple and cinnamon, and there's always a pot simmering on the hob. Yes, nature got it all worked out. The earth mother engaged in food pairing long before the word was invented. Everything you need for a tasty game dish is, after all, widely available at this time of year: mushrooms, chestnuts, cabbage, turnips … they go with game like a hand in a glove. The deep earthy flavours of mushrooms and seasonal vegetables, the sweet accents of the ripe fruit and the spicy aroma of crunchy nuts go hand in hand with the generous promise of fresh game. Breeding and crop produce, however refined they may be, are no match for the natural nobility of ingredients where man has not intervened.

A fine cut of venison or a hearty leg of hare will automatically get the juices flowing, and the choices are endless. The time of heavy sauces is over, and even though the meat may be a little pink, the accompanying drinks should be complementary.
This is the season of freshly baked bread, fragrant pies and warm fruit compotes. You would wax lyrical for less. Somewhere in the distance, you can hear a dog barking.
Fog dampens the peal of the bells, and permeating above this pastoral cantata is the powerful aroma of woodsmoke and damp herbs.

Soft roll with game pasty, pumpkin chutney and Kapittel Pater dressing

Preparation the day before

1 carrot
1 shallot
35 cl Kapittel Pater
10 cl Armagnac
10 juniper berries
sprig of thyme
1 clove of garlic

- Cut the carrot and shallot into chunks, place them in a bowl and pour over the beer and Armagnac. Add the juniper berries, thyme and garlic.
- Place the meat in the marinade and make sure it is totally submerged (add some beer, if necessary). Leave to marinate in a cool place for 12 hours.

Preparation on the day

800 g game ragu
(wild boar, deer or pheasant)
250 g non-prepared minced pork
250 g ground pork throat
1 egg
60 g pistachio nuts
(coarsely chopped)
slices of smoked bacon
to line the terrine
1 terrine mould

- Remove the meat from the marinade.
- Grind half of the meat and cut the other half into 1cm cubes.
- Mix the game with the minced pork, the pork throat, the egg and the pistachio nuts.
  Season with salt and pepper.
- Line the terrine with the bacon and spoon the mixture into it.
  Press the meat down and cover with baking paper.
- Bake the terrine in a bain-marie for 2 hours in the oven at 160 °C.
- Leave the terrine to cool down and set in the refrigerator.
  Drain excess liquid.

Pumpkin and shallot chutney

750 g pumpkin flesh
1 dl olive oil
300 g caster sugar
1 red pepper
2 cloves of garlic
20 g chopped ginger
½ dl white wine vinegar
1 tsp curry powder

- Peel the pumpkin, deseed and cut the pumpkin flesh into 1cm cubes.
- Mix with olive oil, spread the mixture on a baking tray and roast in the oven at 220 °C.
- Allow the sugar to caramelise with a little water and add the finely chopped red pepper, shredded garlic and ginger.
  Deglaze the caramel with white wine vinegar and stir in the curry powder.
- Scoop the roasted pumpkin in the caramel and leave to cook for another 2 minutes. Season with salt and pepper.
- Decant the chutney into a jar and leave to cool (has a long shelf life in the refrigerator).

Dressing

2 egg yolks
1 tbsp of white wine vinegar
5 cl Kapittel Pater
6 cl olive oil
1 tsp mustard

- Beat the yolks with the beer, vinegar and mustard and gently stir in the olive oil.

Presentation

1 small soft, sweet roll per person
a few rocket leaves
1 tsp cranberry jam per person

- Cut open the roll and top with a few rocket leaves.
- Arrange 2 slices of terrine on the lettuce, place the lid on a tilt on the meat and drizzle the dressing around it
- Spoon some chutney and cranberries next to it.
  Sprinkle some chopped pistachio nuts on the plate.

Beer Pairing tip

Kapittel Pater
Van Eecke Brewery, Watou
Abbey Beer

Thirst quencher. Slightly sweet malt aroma, slightly bitter with hints of caramel and liquorice. This modest introduction to the autumn showcases the rich range of aromas that are waiting to make their debut.

Fillet of polder hare with winter vegetables and Tsjeeses Reserva

Preparation the day before

- 2 hare backs with bone
- 50 g butter
- 1 tsp tomato puree
- 1 onion
- 1 carrot
- 1 sprig of thyme
- 1 bay leaf
- 1 tbsp cranberries
- 1 clove of garlic
- 5 cl Tsjeeses Reserva
- 1 l water
- 10 cl cream

- Cut the meat from the carcasses, leaving you with 4 nice fillets.
- Chop up the carcasses and braise them well in butter.
  Add the tomato puree and cook briefly. Add the chopped vegetables, the herbs, the cranberries and garlic to the carcasses and allow to colour further. Douse the stew with the beer and add water until everything is submerged. Bring to the boil and leave the fond to simmer for 2 hours.
- Pour the fond through a sieve and reduce the liquid to half its original volume.

Preparation on the day

- Brown the fillets in butter, remove them from the pan and bake for another 3 minutes in the oven at 180 °C.
- Remove the meat from the oven, cover with aluminium foil and leave to rest in a warm place.
- Deglaze the pan with the fond and reduce the sauce to half its original volume.
- Decant a third of the sauce into a separate plan, add the cream and reduce to the desired thickness.
- Reduce the remainder of the sauce, and season with salt and pepper.

Vegetable garnish

- 1 beetroot
- 1 tbsp white wine vinegar
- 2 salsify
- 4 truffle potatoes
- 1 parsnip
- 25 g butter
- 50 g peas

- Put on your kitchen gloves to handle the beetroot and peel the salsify!
- Cook the beetroot for ½ hour in salted water with a dash of vinegar.
  Peel the beetroot and cut into large chunks.
- Wash the salsify thoroughly, peel and cut into large chunks.
- Do the same with the parsnip and potatoes.
- Put the salsify, parsnip and potatoes in a saucepan filled with salted water.
  Cook for 5 minutes.
- Remove the vegetables from the water and pan-fry them in some butter.
  Season with salt and pepper. Allow the vegetables to cook for 5 minutes under the lid over a low heat.
- Just before serving, add the beetroot cubes and the peas.
  Allow these to heat up briefly.

Presentation

- Spoon the vegetables onto a hot plate.
- Cut the fillets in a fan shape, spread them on the vegetables and drizzle the 2 sauces, neatly separated, over the meat.

Beer Pairing tip

Tsjeeses Reserva
De Struise Brouwers Brewery, Oostvleteren
Strong Amber-coloured winter beer

Strength and character without any flashy ambitions.

Brabant Pheasant with Poperings Hommelbier

Preparation

2 pheasants
1 onion
½ l brown fond
(see polder hare fillet p. 132)
10 cl Poperings Hommel Beer
4 heads of soil-grown chicory
12 Brussels sprouts
50 g smoked bacon cubes
50 g butter
nutmeg

- Remove the fillets and the legs/wings from the pheasants.
- Brown the legs/wings and finely chopped onion in butter, moisten with beer and brown fond and leave to simmer for 2 hours.
- Boil the heads of chicory briefly in salted water, squeeze them to remove any excess liquid and brown them all round in a knob of butter.
- Grate the sprouts on the grater. Pan-fry the bacon and add the grated sprouts. Season with salt, pepper and nutmeg.
- Brown the fillets in hot butter and leave them to cook for a further 4 minutes in the oven at 180°C. Allow them to rest briefly in a warm place.
- Remove the legs/wings from the liquid and cut through the joints (we discarded the bottom section). Keep them warm and reduce the liquid to the desired thickness.

Presentation

- Spoon some sprouts on a hot plate and arrange the top piece of the bone on top.
- Cut the fillet into slices and arrange the meat in a fan shape alongside the sprouts.
- Place a head of chicory on the plate.
- Finish off with the sauce.

Beer Pairing tip

Poperings Hommelbier
Van Eecke Brewery, Watou
Hoppy Blond Beer

Bitter + carbonated: ideally suited as an aperitif (similar to a campari soda or gin & tonic)
Very refreshing hops. High level of bitterness and floral hop aromas.
Produced on the same land, the flavours are in perfect balance.

Beer Pairing tip

Vleteren Alt
Deca Brewery, Woesten
Dark Ale

Slightly sweet with a hint of caramel, wood and gingerbread.
A trace of dark chocolate in the aftertaste. The complex sweetness in the glass allows the dark sensation of the meat to explode.

Wild duck with turnips, carrots and honey in Vleteren Alt

2 wild ducks
40 g butter
15 cl Vleteren Alt
50 cl brown fond
2 turnips
2 carrots
1 tbsp honey
4 sprigs of watercress

Preparation

- Remove the fillets and legs/wings from the carcass. Brown the legs/wings in some butter and douse them with the beer and the fond. Allow to simmer for ½ hour, remove the legs/wings from the gravy, strain the gravy and reduce to sauce thickness.
- Peel the carrots and the turnips, cut them into pieces and sauté them in 25 grammes of butter and some water and honey under a lid until they are *al dente*.
- Brown the fillets on both sides in browned butter (skin side first). Allow them to bake for another 3 minutes in the oven at 180 °C and let them rest for 10 minutes.

Presentation

- Slice the fillet and arrange on a warm plate.
- Spoon the sauce in between.
- Arrange the pieces of carrot and turnip on the plate and finish off with a sprig of watercress.
- You may want to serve some potato gratin with this dish.

Sushi of wild boar fillet, cep, pumpkin strips and horseradish cream marinated in Reninge Old Brown

Wild boar fillet and cep

300 g wild boar fillet
1 bottle of Reninge Old Brown
3 tbsp honey
200 g cep
25 g butter
1 clove of garlic
1 tbsp white wine vinegar
100 g sushi rice
1 sushi mat
extra beer for reducing
4 fine strips of crisply fried bacon

- Make a marinade with the honey and half of the beer and allow the meat to rest in it for a few hours.
- Remove the meat from the marinade, pat it dry and grill it all round under the grill to form a crust. Wrap the hot fillet in cling film and tighten it well so that the flavours of the marinade and the grilled crust can infuse into the meat.
- Cut the cep into small pieces and pan-fry in a knob of butter. Season with salt and pepper and the crushed garlic. Moisten it with the rest of the beer and the white wine vinegar. Boil the rice in this.
- Cut the meat into thin slices lengthwise. Place it on the sushi mat and spread some rice on top. Roll up the meat with the rice in the mat and leave the rolls to rest for a while in the refrigerator. Cut them into portions.
- Reduce the beer to a caramel-like consistency.

Pumpkin strips

150 g pumpkin flesh
3 tbsp olive oil
1 tbsp white wine vinegar
coarse see salt

- Make a marinade of the olive oil, white wine vinegar, sea salt and black ground pepper.
- Cut the pumpkin flesh with a grater into thin slivers and let them marinate for an hour. In a closed jar, this preparation has a long shelf life in the refrigerator.

Horseradish cream

1 horseradish
10 cl cream
2 tbsp mayonnaise

- Peel the horseradish and grate finely.
- Mix with the cream and mayonnaise.

Presentation

- Make a bed of pumpkin strips and cover these with 3 sushi and a strip of smoked bacon.
- Pipe a few blobs of horseradish cream on the plate.
- Finish off with drops of beer caramel.

Beer Pairing tip

Reninge Old Brown
Seizoensbrouwerij Vandewalle, Lo-Reninge
Flemish Old Brown

Caramel-bitter, tart taste with dark roasted malt and demerara. Style and class face-to-face with tradition and innovation. An Old Brown as a mischievous chaperone.

De Beauvoordse Walhoeve
Veurne

Verstraete
Diksmuide

De Dolle Brouwers Brewery
Esen

Malt and Brewery House De Snoek
Alveringem

Vandewalle Seasonal Brewery
Lo-Reninge

De Struise Brouwers Brewery
Oostvleteren

Sint-Sixtus Brewery
Westvleteren

Deca Brewery
Woesten

't Hoppecruyt
Poperinge (Proven)

Van Eecke Brewery
Watou

St. Bernardus Brewery
Watou

La maison Flandre pigeonneau
Steenvoorde (FR)

De Lovie
Poperinge

De Plukker Brewery
Poperinge

Watch and Do Farm den Overdraght
Poperinge

Het Sas Brewery
Boezinge

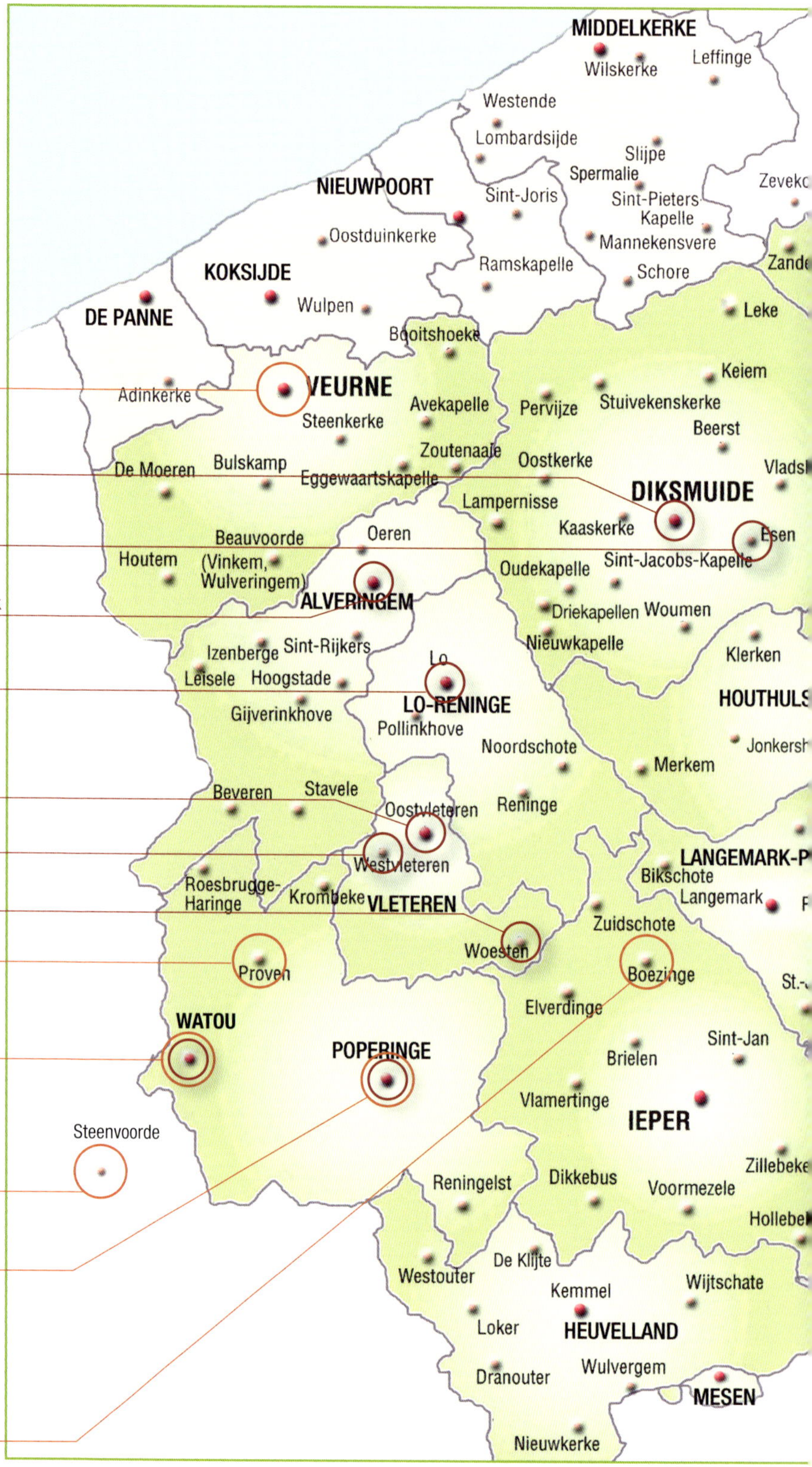

Flanders' Fields

Traditional? Of course!

Traditional goes hand in hand with small-scale, which, in turn, stands for top quality and maximum transparency. The company and producers featured in this book do not only score on 'Open Day for Companies' for the doors only close at night. From stable to meatball, from malt to stout beer, from barley to plate ... all the ingredients are 100% traceable.

Flanders' Fields reads like an open book: nothing in the pockets, nothing up our sleeves, just honest food!

Index

Acknowledgements

This book feels good. In fact, it feels wonderful, because it is a reflection of 30 years of commitment, 30 years of enthusiasm. My thanks go first to those who believed in me: the many employees who have given the best of themselves, and continue to do so, to make 't Hommelhof the culinary hangout which it has become today.
Thank you to all good friends and loyal customers who were there in the good days and the bad. Without their loyalty, this story would never be told. Thanks, finally, to publishing house Stichting Kunstboek, photographer Tom Swijns, author Jan Dhondt and Simon who each have given the best in their field.
A grateful, proud father,
Stefaan

Recipes

Stefaan Couttenye

Beer Pairing suggestions

Simon Couttenye

Text

Jan Dhondt

Photography

Tom Swijns

Translation

Taal-Ad-Visie

Editing

Hilde Deweer

Lay-out and styling

Group Van Damme, Oostkamp

Printed by

PurePrint, Oostkamp

Published by

Stichting Kunstboek bvba
Legeweg 165
B-8020 Oostkamp
T. +32 (0)50 46 19 10
F. +32 (0)50 46 19 18
info@stichtingkunstboek.com
www.stichtingkunstboek.com

't Hommelhof
Watouplein 17
B-8978 Watou
T. +32 (0)57 38 80 24
www.hommelhof.be

ISBN 978-90-5856-483-2
NUR: 440
D/2014/6407/12